KV-590-662

ACTIVATING PARTICIPATION:
PARENTS AND TEACHERS WORKING
TOWARDS PARTNERSHIP

edited by
Gill Crozier and Diane Reay

Trentham Books
Stoke on Trent, UK and Sterling, USA

University of Plymouth
Library

Item No

9006400446

Shelfmark

370.34 ACT

Trentham Books Limited
Westview House   22883 Quicksilver Drive
734 London Road   Sterling
Oakhill   VA 20166-2012
Stoke on Trent   USA
Staffordshire
England ST4 5NP

© 2005 Gill Crozier and Diane Reay

All rights reserved. No part of this publication may be
reproduced or transmitted in any form or by any means,
electronic or mechanical including photocopying, recording or
any information storage or retrieval system, without prior
permission in writing from the publishers.

First published 2005

British Library Cataloguing-in-Publication Data
A catalogue record for this book is available from the
British Library

ISBN-13: 978-1-85856-325-1
ISBN-10: 1-85856-325-9

Designed and typeset by Trentham Print Design Ltd., Chester
and printed in Great Britain by Cromwell Press Ltd,
Trowbridge.

Acknowledgements

We would like to thank Year 6 (2003-4) children of Walkergate Primary
School, Newcastle Upon Tyne for drawing pictures for the book cover and
Amy Bambro whose picture was chosen.

We would also like to thank Gillian Klein of Trentham Books for her
editorial comments and advice.

The chapters comprising this collection are based on papers originally
presented as part of an ESRC funded seminar series (Ref: 451 264 952 99)
2000-2002 entitled Parents and Schools: Diversity, Participation and
Democracy.

Contents

Notes on contributors

Gill Crozier is Professor of Education at the University of Sunderland. Her research interests include home-school relations, the school experiences of young people, urban education and social justice issues. She is currently directing the ESRC project: Parents and Schools: Asian Families' Perspectives. Her publications include: *Parents and Schools: Partners or Protagonists?* (2000 Trentham Books).

Miriam E David is Professor of Policy Studies in Education and Dean of Research in the Faculty of Humanities and Social Sciences at Keele University. She has an international reputation for her research on education, family, gender and policy sociology. Her latest book *Personal and Political: Feminisms, Sociology and Family Lives* was published by Trentham Books in 2003

Maggie MacLure is Professor of Education at Manchester Metropolitan University. She is interested in educational discourses and in research methodology. She is the author of *Discourse in Educational and Social Research* (2003 Open University Press).

Dr Jane Martin is the executive director of the Centre for Public Scrutiny, a new organisation established to promote understanding of public scrutiny in effective government, and an honorary research fellow at the University of Birmingham, School of Education. She also has experience as a local authority education officer and a management consultant. Recent research includes the ESRC Democracy and Participation programme project 'School Governors as Active Citizens'. She co-authored the joint Improvement and Development Agency and New Local Government Network publication with Liz Allen 'Governing Education for Community Regeneration'. Her recent book with Ann Holt '*Joined Up Governance*' is a good practice guide for lay school governors.

Heidi Safia Mirza is Professor of Racial Equality Studies at Middlesex University. She is known internationally for her work on ethnicity, gender and identity in education with best selling books such as *Young, Female, and Black, and Black British Feminism*. As a member of the Labour Government's *Schools'*

Standards Task Force she helped shape many initiatives to do with raising standards in education for black and minority ethnic pupils. Recently she has been appointed to the Equality Challenge for Universities UK, spearheading the drive for diversity in higher education. She has established the Runnymede Collection at Middlesex, a unique race-relations archive and library, documenting the late 20th Century civil rights struggle for a Multicultural Britain.

Dr Jane Ribbens McCarthy is a Lecturer in the Faculty of Social Sciences at the Open University. Her long-term research interests have centred on the sociology of family lives, particularly in relation to parents and children. She has published extensively in this area; her most recent book is '*Making Families: Moral Tales of Parenting and Step-Parenting*', (with Rosalind Edwards and Val Gillies), (2003 Sociology Press). She is currently researching relationships disrupted by bereavement, with a book in progress on 'Young People's Experiences of Loss and Bereavement: Towards an Interdisciplinary Approach', (2005 forthcoming, Open University Press).

Anne Phillips is Professor of Gender Theory at the London School of Economics, and has written extensively on gender, equality, and democracy. Her publications include *Engendering Democracy* (Polity 1991), *The Politics of Presence* (OUP, 1995) and *Which Equalities Matter?* (Polity Press, 1999. She is currently working on issues of gender and cultural diversity.

Diane Reay is Professor of Sociology of Education at the Institute for Policy Studies in Education at London Metropolitan University. Her research interests include gender, race and social class inequalities in education, social and educational segregation in inner cities, Bourdieu's social theory and children's experiences of schooling. Her forthcoming book (with Stephen Ball and Miriam David) is *Degrees of Choice: social class, race and gender in higher education* (Trentham Books).

Dr Carol Vincent is a senior lecturer in education policy at the Institute of Education. Her research interests include home-school relations, social justice, childcare and social class. She is currently directing an ESRC project on choice and provision of pre-school childcare. Her latest book is an edited collection, '*Social Justice, Education and Identity*' (2003, RoutledgeFalmer).

Dr Barbara M Walker is a lecturer in the Centre for Applied Research in Education at the University of East Anglia. Her current research interests include home-school liaison, creativity in school and the community, and the acquisition of gender identity. Recent publications include: (2002) 'The Missing Person: student roles in home-school interviews' *European Educational Research Journal*, 2 (3) 468-479, and (2004) 'Frames of Self: capturing working class British boys' identities through photographs' in J. Chu and N. Way (Eds) *Adolescent Boys in Context* (New York: New York University Press)

Introduction

Gill Crozier and Diane Reay

The statement by the then Secretary of State for Education David Blunkett that parents are a child's primary educator (DfEE, 1997) is well known. However, since then Government has never, seemingly, been convinced that parents were pulling their weight with respect to their children's education. For example there was legislation which threatened to – and subsequently did – imprison parents whose children were repeatedly late for school or didn't attend at all (Gillan, 2002). More recently we have the Anti-Social Behaviour Act (2003), to cover extended absences and truancy. In addition we saw the introduction of parenting classes both on a voluntary basis and as a punishment for such putative misdemeanours. Not only does this suggest a lack of trust in parents but also it infantilises the parent, treating her/him (and as we will see later most often it is her) like the child. Parents are treated as a homogeneous group; no account is taken of gender, social class or ethnic differences and the possible constraints upon their ability and opportunity to ensure perfect behaviour from their children and ideal parenting by themselves. The parents who have been identified in the media and by ministers as wanting in these ways are lone mothers, the economically disadvantaged, sometimes with drug related problems (Ahmed and Bright, 2002; Gillan, 2002; Dyer, 2003).

From the growing body of research into home-school relations we know that parents who find it most difficult to be involved in a relationship with their child's school and act on their child's behalf in relation to the school are white working class and black and minority ethnic group parents. A new discourse is emerging around 'hard to reach families' which takes a less punitive stance than as represented by the legislation referred to above but sets apart these families as different and implies a sense of inadequacy. Such parents are urged for example to take parenting lessons.

None of these strategies, we argue here, is helpful in developing equitable participation and dialogue. Indeed the strategies whereby parents are enabled to engage with teachers about their children's education are absent; so is any policy which involves parents in presenting their views about for example pedagogy and the nature of the curriculum. The chapters in this volume explore the extent of parents' involvement in their children's education but also show that they are not or cannot be, for a variety of reasons, as yet democratically participative. They challenge the successive insinuations that parents generally and mothers in particular don't care. But they also show the difficulties that parents face in trying on the one hand to meet the demands or at least expectations of schools and trying to assert a voice on behalf of their children, and on the other, protecting a private space for themselves and their families. This book reveals the competitiveness and its impact between parents, intentionally or otherwise.

The book does not present a set of answers nor a blueprint for achieving the perfect partnership. In fact we don't think such a thing exists. The make-up, organisation social and economic context and the client group of schools differs on a school by school basis. These considerations affect the nature of home-school relations and what both parents and schools can do about this. The chapters in this book explore the complexity of these issues and hopefully provide insights which will enable teachers and other educationalists and also parents to develop participatory strategies which are meaningful to their own circumstances.

This book explores the issues surrounding the arguments for an inclusive form of involvement by parents. By this we mean a form of involvement that supports and promotes participation defined as much by the parents and children themselves as the schools and teachers. In this way we believe participation can become more meaningful and productive. However, participation in this sense raises some challenging issues such as equality, the right to a voice, democracy and accountability; the tension in power relationships between parents and teachers and the potential challenge to teacher professionalism. In addition parental participation raises issues of boundaries and the blurring of these between home and school and the implications of crossing them or not.

Although 'parental involvement' is frequently referred to in policy discourses and professional practice few are explicit about what they actually mean. Nevertheless researchers have identified various typologies of 'parental involvement' (Vincent, 1996; Tomlinson, 1991; Epstein, 1990) clearly demonstrating the range and variability of parents' work in relation to school. We are not concerned here with a specific type of 'parental involvement'. Our premise is based on the role of parents as supporters of and advocates for their children and as having the knowledge and understanding to ensure the most effective and positive educational experience possible for their children. Therefore, we recognise the importance of dialogue and action between teachers and parents that would enable parents to have a significant voice in making appropriate decisions that impact on their children's educational experience. Issues surrounding the challenge for both teachers and the parents themselves in achieving such inclusion are explored, together with the identification of some strategies for further action outlined in the concluding chapter.

The chapters arise from an ESRC funded seminar series[1] which was held across five universities between 2000 and 2002 and involved academics, practitioners, and parents. The book is structured in three sections. In the first section, Parental Involvement: the implications of gender, 'race' and class, the experiences of mothers and issues relating to social class and 'race' are identified as key factors in influencing parents' participation. Chapter 1 *Activating Participation: A Personal Reflection on Research on Mothers and Education* by Miriam David presents some of the issues facing mothers in their relationship with schools and the education service, together with an analysis of the significance of the criticisms of mothers implicit in the policies on parental activities and responsibilities. The chapter provides an overview of research into mothers' involvement over a number of years. The extensive nature of mothering practices are demonstrated.

Not all such practices are equitable or are in the interests of all mothers, fathers or children. In *Mothers' Involvement in their Children's Schooling: Social Reproduction in Action?* (Chapter 2) Diane Reay develops a discussion of the role of mothers in relation to social reproduction and the ways powerful mothers, as involved parents, can undermine the effectiveness of less powerful mothers. It also outlines the ways in which powerful mothers can set the 'standard' of behaviour that comes to be expected by teachers.

In Chapter 3 *Beyond the Call of Duty: the impact of racism on black parents' involvement in their children's education*, Gill Crozier presents an analysis of the ways that black parents (particularly mothers) engage in the support, defence and protection of their children in the face of a system that is failing to meet their children's needs. It demonstrates the extensive emotional labour that mothers and to some extent fathers engage in, in addition to the domestic labour (providing meals, the school uniform, and resources; ensuring the child gets to school on time), and professional labour (labour expended in supporting the homework, listening to the reading; providing educational experiences out of the home) that is more clearly understood even though not always recognised.

In section 2, Participatory Democracy: 'no one said it would be easy' a range of issues around developing parental participation are explored. In particular some of the chapters question the desirablility of home-school links and parental participation in terms of how they tend to be constructed. What is or maybe possible and what influences such participation? In Chapter 4, *Negotiating Public and Private: Maternal Mediations of Home-School Boundaries*, Jane Ribbens McCarthy presents the concepts of public and private alongside that of the personal. She explores the use of these theoretical concepts in a consideration of the lives of mothers in the context of home-school relations. Her focus is that of the home and she raises the question of how far there is scope for mothers to build on their privately based experiences to resist dominant discourses and organisational imperatives around the schooling of their children. We see how some mothers are wearied by the demands of the school but Ribbens McCarthy also discusses the whole issue of the colonisation of the home by the school and she argues for boundary maintenance.

Anne Phillips, in *Participation, Inequality, Self-interest* (Chapter 5), draws on political philosophy to explore the question of equality and parental participation in schools and whether it could ever be achievable. Phillips discusses a range of theoretical issues relating to questions of participation, representation and deliberation. She focuses on forms of participation that may enable parents to influence school policy and practice; these forms include involvement in school governing bodies and parent-teacher associations. However, the issues of inequality in participatory opportunities and the problem for schools of engaging with diverse parental groups – their values, beliefs and needs, are central here. The issues discussed are around educational knowledge, experience and self confidence in the face of professionals/experts as actual or potential constraints, together with those of time, inflexible jobs, childcare demands, and the success achieved for some at the expense of others.

Chapter 6, *Home-School Partnerships in Practice*, takes the example of parents' evening and examines a number of interactional problems which shed some light on the barriers between the different protagonists. This chapter draws on two research projects undertaken by Barbara Walker and Maggie Maclure which investigated secondary school parents' evenings. In a policy climate which has promoted parental choice, accountability and shared responsibility between home and school for children's educational and social development, the authors argue that the annual parents' evening is a key event, at least symbolically. The chapter describes and analyses encounters between parents, teachers and children that took place within this parents' evening format.

Section 3 looks at Participation in Action. The previous discussions are harnessed and potential avenues of and strategies for change are identified. In Chapter 7 *Parents as citizens: making the case*, Carol Vincent and Jane Martin consider the following questions: what is the role of parents in relation to schools and the education system as a whole? What is a desirable role? What is feasible? What is appropriate? They recognise that answers will be different depending on the identity of the individual parent. The chapter begins by looking at some of the current responses to these questions by drawing on recent research literature, policy and practice. In the second part of the chapter the authors begin to shape their own answers, arguing that there is a role for parents as citizens in their interactions with the education system; notwithstanding the partiality and fragility of this role.

Interestingly, where parents have a democratic opportunity of expressing their views, participating, even when it may still be hard work, seems to be a possibility. In Chapter 8, *Doing Parental Participation Differently: Black Women's Participation as Educators and Mothers in Black Supplementary Schooling*, Diane Reay and Heidi Safia Mirza look at an alternative parental participation strategy. Drawing on a small scale study this chapter presents a discussion of black women's educational involvement through the supplementary school movement. Reay and Mirza argue that supplementary schools represent spaces of radical blackness. They also demonstrate how parents can be involved effectively where there is a commitment and willingness to enable this, even when teachers and parents hold different educational philosophies.

Chapter 9 concludes by drawing together the issues raised and identifying the main themes to emerge across the chapters. It also presents some strategies to answer the questions raised. Whilst recognising the impossibility of solving wider social inequalities through the education system, the chapter considers what is feasible within specific educational contexts.

Note

1 ESRC Seminar Competition Series R451 264 952 99

SECTION 1
Parental Involvement: the implications of gender, 'race' and class

1

Activating Participation:
a personal reflection on research
on mothers and education

Miriam E. David

Introduction

n this chapter I want to reflect upon my personal and professional academic developments as a sociologist in relation to
those of others pursuing similar themes about mothers and
education in Britain and the wider international community of
feminist scholars concerned about equity and social justice. What
I argue is that research on families, especially parents, and schools,
or home-school relations, has changed in relation to both transformations in the wider social and political contexts, and the ways
in which we, as feminists, sociologists and social scientists, have
tried to understand and transform those changing developments
in family and education. Moreover, there have been a number of
critical events, especially changes in the political, policy and social
contexts that have been influential in the complex ways in which
understandings and social and familial changes have occurred.
Thus research on parents and schools, home-school relations and/
or parental participation in education, has become more than substantive topics. The notions have been deconstructed and transformed into theoretical and methodological issues about families

and education. They have also contributed to more active ways of constructing, as well as deconstructing, notions of participation, community and democracy.

The approach that I take here is that of intellectual biography and using the feminist methodologies of reflections, biographies or autobiography and 'memoirs' (Stanley, 1992) as they have been adopted in the academy (David, 2002; 2003). The chapter was originally based upon several presentations and papers[1] that reviewed and reflected upon feminist and collaborative research on families, gender and education over the last 30 years and that explored the contributions that feminist academic scholarship, theories and methodologies made to understanding and changing the wider social and political contexts.

Since it was presented three years ago, I have completed and published a book *Personal and Political: Feminisms, Sociology and Family Life* (2003) that is a much wider project of writing about feminisms, sociology and family lives in a personal and reflexive vein. Thus the chapter now draws upon my wider reflections upon the ways in which feminist politics or activism has become entwined with wider political strategies and academic, theoretical and methodological developments. In the book I argue that there have been three distinctive policy regimes around forms of liberalism, and that feminist theories in the academy have developed in relation to these global social and political transformations.

The first era was of social democracy or liberalism, linked to postwar social changes and economic growth. This was an era of development of social movements including the women's liberation movement, and socialist and civil rights movements. I considered the ways in which second wave feminism developed approaches to feminist politics, theories and pedagogies as feminism entered the academy. These were intertwined with early second wave feminists' struggles to achieve social change and sexual equality and also to transform their own family lives and create alternate ways of living. The slogan 'the personal is political' became the rallying call of feminist activists. It was the notion that personal matters in the family were in fact not private and individual but related deeply and significantly to wider political issues and power relations between men and women in public life, in employment and political activities.

Exploring questions about family life, and especially mothers, mothering and motherhood has not always been fashionable amongst feminists and has indeed been seen as either essentialist or traditionalist. Creating alternative ways of living amongst feminists was an attempt to move away from the traditional patriarchal nuclear family and explore sex, sexuality, gender, generation and alternative child-rearing and educational methods. However, as feminists developed research, theories and methodologies within the academy, together with the work of other social scientists, these have focused broadly on families and education not only as substantive topics but also as theoretical and methodological issues.

The second era, which has recently been called economic liberalism, was a period associated with transformations in the economy and polity towards markets and a backlash over both political activism and theoretical understandings. Nevertheless, this period may be considered as one in which feminist theories and methodologies had become firmly embedded within the academy internationally. Thus feminist scholarship began to flourish in the disciplines and develop distinctive characteristics, more associated with different disciplines and subjects. Here the notion that the personal was linked with the political in complex and detailed ways began to characterise new forms of feminist scholarship and theory and diverge from feminist political activities outside the academy.

The third era can be considered to be that of neo-liberalism, as Nancy Fraser (1997) has called it, in trying to link what she calls the post-socialist condition with wider feminist and complex theoretical understandings of global and social transformations. This period may be characterised by what could be considered to be a transformation in feminist understandings and methodologies to more personal considerations. Thus the method of personal reflection and notions about self-analysis and critical reflections have come to dominate the social sciences, with what has been dubbed 'the biographic turn', as have ideas about reflexivity.

It is possible to see this period of academic and feminist theorising about family matters as about how the political is personal; how public agendas and activities are suffused with questions of the personal, the intimate and private. Questions of participation, community and democracy turn on issues to do with personal and intimate involvements rather than broader more social questions. Thus over the last 25 to 30 years there have been rich and varied developments in our perspectives and understandings, in which the methodologies of personal reflections and reflexivity have become paramount.

Perspectives

There are five perspectives that I thread through this account about the ways in which the wider social and political context influenced emerging perspectives on family, mothers and education. These link with the three policy regimes that I outlined above. What I also want to argue is that theoretical and methodological approaches changed as bodies of knowledge developed about parents and schools or home-school relations. The first perspective is that of the development of feminist scholarship in the academy about family and education, drawing on traditional social scientific approaches and studies but in which relations between the sexes were highlighted. The second perspective was about how feminists developed changing theories about family life and linked studies of families to a wider context as part of the developing disciplines of sociology, family sociology and sociology of education. These two perspectives were developed within the first social liberal regime. The third perspective drew on developing social theories and methodologies to inform substantive and empirical studies of mothers' positioning in/through education at all levels from early childhood through to higher education. This is linked to the second policy regime and this also shades into the fourth. The fourth perspective was about how these developed into critical policy analyses and evaluations of policy developments, particularly changing policy contexts, highlighting gender, class and 'race', and their implications for women's lives and personal experiences. This and the fifth perspective are clearly associated with theoretical, methodological and substantive diversity, in particular in relation to feminist and post-structural ways of thinking and relate to the third policy regime of neo-liberalism. The fifth perspective is about how these notions developed into wider theoretical explanations for social and familial changes more recently and their implications for gender equity and social justice, and particularly attempts to inform community and political participation and democracy.

Feminist personal reflections and changing methodologies

As early second wave feminists have become established, if not fully accepted as part of the academy, many of them have begun to reflect back upon their personal and professional lives and the development of their scholarship, theories and methodologies. This kind of writing of intellectual biography and considering the origins and antecedents of theoretical and methodological developments has become fashionable, respectable and, indeed, *de rigeur* and much of the auto/biography has focused on aspects of family life. The feminist credo of 'the personal is political' was dominant during the early period and was an attempt to argue that intimate questions about being a woman, a daughter, a mother, a sister and about sexuality were not only personal and particular but also more public and political. These notions became more widespread as others in both social movements and as academics, particularly as social scientists, began to consider how to understand social transformations. Understandings of the relations between personal and political, and private and public matters, especially in relation to family and education, have become a critical theme in more recent studies. These have transformed the notion of 'the personal is political' to that of the 'political being personal'.

Like many women of my generation who became involved in the women's liberation movement in the late 1960s, it was initially an activity that I engaged with as a political movement for social and policy changes, new forms of democratic participation, rather than as a professional and academic activity. Feminist ideas have often had to be only part of my personal and political rather than professional life, except that such ideas have influenced the ways in which material was chosen in the academic context. In the early

1970s at Bristol University we, as a generation and group of feminists, slowly began to introduce feminist political activities and studies into the academy and with great difficulty as they were not acceptable as serious scholarship and were outside the disciplines. It is only in the last 25 years that feminist scholarship has developed within the discipline of sociology, and the other social sciences.

For instance, I became a member of the Bristol Women's Studies Group (BWSG) which wrote the first introduction to women's studies (1979; 1984). At that time, we were interested in the ideas about how our family and personal lives linked with our broader political interests as young women seeking social and sexual changes or what was then 'women's liberation'. Some of us were married and/or cohabiting and had very young children; others had sexual relationships of a more open-ended kind, despite the constrictions imposed by limited laws and policies on 'family planning' or abortion and contraception and sexual orientation. We all wished to explore how sexual and familial relationships impacted upon and influenced our wider activities and we began to consider these issues in a broad educational context, for extramural rather than undergraduate courses. At that time there was very little material available and we gathered together ephemeral accounts as material for the book and for our classes, where personal accounts of family lives were also the key material.

Four years ago, we held a twentieth anniversary party when we indulged in reflections on our changing personal and family lives and how feminism, theories and methodologies had entered the academy and the disciplines. In particular Marilyn Porter, who was a member of the BSWG and participant at the anniversary celebrations has, together with her daughter, Fenella, produced an intriguing example of a changing generational emphasis in feminist academic writing and activities. Their mother-daughter collaboration is an instance of how writing auto/biographically and exploring 'voices' and narratives develops feminist theory and methodologies (Marilyn and Fenella Porter, 1999). It is a rich account of feminist theory now used as pedagogy within the academy.

Developing research topics on mothers, families and education

At the same time as becoming involved in feminist politics and activities at arms' length from the academy, I also began to try and develop a more historical and theoretical approach to my sociological work as a teacher within the academy. I was drawn to this in part through my feminist colleagues and our developing interests in what we began to call courses in family and social policy. This was also partly personal; opportunities and constraints from my family background, since my mother was a schoolteacher and both my parents deeply interested in education. Thus I tried to develop links with topics to do with own family and education. It was also about trying to imbue academic work with questions of social and sexual equality and urgent issues of social change (to paraphrase Hartsock, 1998).

Initially I explored these interests historically and comparatively through *The State, Family and Education* published in 1980. Here I attempted to bring together a socialist analysis with feminism. At that time French Marxist theory was fashionable and I pursued a feminist analysis of what Althusser had named as 'the family-education couple', that is the links between family and education as ideological state apparatuses or through state policies and 'regulation'. In keeping with the theoretical developments of the time, I saw both family and education as social institutions and focused the relations between the sexes in the historical developments of schooling and teaching as a profession. I also explored the ways in which the state regulated the relations between parents and schools. This built upon other, non-feminist studies of parents and schools, many of which drew upon emerging ideas about participation and democracy as themes within education and schools. These other studies did not deconstruct notions of family, parent, home or school and education; and did not provide a gendered analysis.

I also began to develop a professional and research agenda related to my own developments on becoming a mother in the late 1970s and linked to the lives of my children. Given the lack of public child care for pre-school and after school children, I became involved with colleagues in campaigning for child care provisions through the university and eventually setting up the University nursery parents' association (UNPA). This committee was given the power and the responsibilities to run a university nursery for pre-school children of students and staff, especially academics.

At the same time, I developed a more intellectual and academic interest in childcare. This resulted in writing, with Caroline New (1985) *For the Children's Sake: Making Child Care More than Women's Business*. We explored theoretically, historically and contemporaneously developments in child care policies and practices, with examples of innovative and alternative, participatory experiments mainly for pre-school children and their early educational developments. We looked at developments in motherhood and fatherhood nationally and internationally from a feminist perspective. We also linked to a developing national campaign in the early 1980s for more generous public provisions for mothers of young children – the National Child Care Campaign. With the benefit of hindsight, it is intriguing to note the connections that the campaigning strategy has had with the New Labour government's initiative in the National Child Care Strategy, almost 20 years later (David, 1999). Since then the strategy has been implemented, linked with Sure Start, creating a network of childcare provisions with local community involvement and parental participation.

Developing feminist analyses on mothers and education or home-school relations

During this time of burgeoning feminist activities and intellectual developments in the late 1970s and early 1980s I was also pushed to explore the complexities of issues for mothers and education by the growing team of colleagues who were mainly postgraduate students, conducting research for doctorates. Initially, some of these conducted studies of aspects of family life theoretically and academically, whilst others explored educational practices. These two and twin interests were only slowly brought together into a joint endeavour that then developed into studies of the complexities of the relations between families and education, including higher education and the academy. This has only begun to assume theoretical and wider methodological importance in the 1990s.

However, three feminist historical studies were important in pointing the way to these later developments. For example, an important study was conducted by Linda Ward on the history of birth control in England in the 1920s, which paralleled a study by Linda Gordon (1980) of birth control in America. She pursued her own interest in how family planning developed in Britain and how early feminists had theorised these developments. Similarly Myna Trustram developed her own interests in relations between the army and public life in a historical study of married women's relation to the army, having grown up in a garrison town and having been distanced from such sexual relations. This was subsequently published as *Women of the Regiment: Marriage and the Victorian Army* (1984). Gill Blunden developed a historical analysis of further education and courses for young women at the turn of the nineteenth century and into the early twentieth century (1983).

Secondly three further studies, all conducted at South Bank rather than Bristol University, began to develop the genre of studies, taking personal experiences as the starting point. Following from Gill Blunden's study and her own earlier interests in adult education for women (Hughes and Kennedy, 1984), Mary Hughes focused on the history and practices of Adult Education, largely for women and mothers at home. Hughes' interests were in the policies and practices of adult education as she herself was an organiser of adult education classes mainly but not exclusively for women.

Ros Edwards, who had herself been a mature mother student, decided to study women like herself and different types of higher education. She was interested in how such women students linked or kept separate their family and educational lives, moving the boundaries of notions about family from those of merely mothers of schoolchildren, to exploring experiences in other contexts. This study was subsequently published in 1993 as *Mature Women Students – Separating or Connecting Family and Education*. Subsequently she has gone on to explore separately and together with other colleagues complex notions of family (Duncan and Edwards, 1997, 1999). She is now engaged a large-scale ESRC-funded research group on Families and Social Capital, based at London South Bank University, and publishes prolifically in these areas.

Jane Ribbens developed her own interests in aspects of family life to do with mothers and their young children in the community rather than linked to school. Drawing on her own experiences as a full-time mother of two young children in a suburban community Ribbens explored child-rearing practices in a middle income community and this was subsequently published as *Mothers and their Children: A feminist sociology of child-rearing* (1994). Her theoretical developments in exploring mothers' experiences of child rearing are legion. They have been critical to the development of theories about the personal, and boundaries between public and private (Ribbens, 2000; Ribbens and Edwards eds, 1997).

Together we developed an early analysis of the issues involved in thinking about mothers and education. Drawing on our individual interests and research studies we brought together our studies in a volume entitled *Mothers and Education: Inside Out? Exploring Family Education Policy and Experience* (1993). We explored both the pleasures and pains of writing about these issues in an increasingly cold political and intellectual climate of the 1980s and early 1990s. We thus drew the conclusion:

> Finally we believe we have found that a feminist set of case studies, from our vantage point, has begun to aid the process of developing clearer understanding and knowledge ... Given that we are all feminists, professionals, academics and mothers who are in mid-career, we have concentrated our attention on these issues of family-education relations. Despite our clear professional and educational differences and careers to date we have all found ourselves in agreement on the problematic issues to do with current home-school or family-education relations ... We also want to find ways to ensure that mothers are not made to feel guilty about their choices in the private sphere of the home or even in public arenas. Motherhood is not only pleasurable in and of itself but is crucially important for future generations, for changes in the balances between home and school, public and private, family and education. Rearing children and constructing the understanding and know-

ledge on which we all come to 'know' the world is as importantly done by mothers in circumstances of their own choosing as it is done by constricting, controlling and confining public agendas which do not acknowledge these issues (1993, p.222-3).

Thirdly, other colleagues and students have begun to contribute to the growing theoretical sophistication of these kinds of feminist studies, of the complexities of the relations between families and education. Moreover, wider feminist theoretical developments linked to sociological theoretical developments have influenced our methodologies. Thus nuanced studies of diverse types of family and of reflecting upon our practices have become more influential. Diane Reay, as a woman from a working class background, who had become a primary schoolteacher and returned to higher education as a mature mother postgraduate student, was also interested in pursuing a study which linked substantively and methodologically with her own expertise and interests. She developed a study comparing a middle class and working class community in relation to mothers' involvement in their primary schoolchildren's education, which compared with Annette Lareau's study in the USA (1989). However, Diane Reay extended that analysis by using a feminist approach carefully linked with Bourdieu's theories and especially his notion of 'habitus'. This has been published as *Class Work: Mothers' Involvement in their Children's Primary Schooling* (1998). She has gone on to develop important analyses of mothers' work and education, including work with Heidi Mirza on Saturday schools as a form of black social movement (2000 see also chapter 8 this volume) and Lucey on working class mothers and children's perspectives on school choice (2000).

Similarly Kay Standing developed an analysis of working class mothers in particular circumstances as lone mothers. From her own background and experiences, she was also interested in exploring particular lone mothers' experiences in relation to their children's education (1997; 1999). These various studies led us to want to reflect more not just on our substantive interests and concerns but also on our various methodological developments. We became keen to explore the developing approaches to reflexivity and how these might be used with our own work. We also tried to develop a comparative research study with Alison Griffith and Dorothy Smith in Canada and the USA, to explore the diverse meanings and understandings of mothering in relation to children's education. However, we found that the different national contexts for schooling and education inhibited the easy and ready translation of their concepts to another country and locale (Smith and Griffith, 1990). We thus wrote about the moral as well as structural constraints on these issues (David *et al*, 1996). We also considered the ways in which policy developments were increasingly beginning to constrain and constrict mothers in their lives with children (David *et al*, 1997).

Policy relevant studies about mothers and education

What was becoming clear in the late 1980s was the extent to which the developments in the British policy context, *inter alia*, were increasingly beginning to constrain mothers and others in relation to children and their education, especially with moves towards increasing marketisation and privatisation of education and schools. In the aftermath of the Education Reform Act 1988 it seemed important to explore precisely how policy and experiences in family and education were changing family practices. I was thus drawn to reconsider the complex ways in which, social and educational reforms were influencing, and being influenced by, the social and economic contexts and changing structures and patterns of family life. The wider social and political transformations led to a revised language or discourse about policy developments. Reform became a substitute for policy, drawing upon shifts and terms from the USA (Fairclough, 2000). In this climate, too, the language of feminist analysis also shifted; increasingly that of gender was substituted, together with the nature of our substantive studies. Accordingly I reviewed the evidence for the changing contexts and policies and their influences on changing experiences and practices (David, 1993). I wrote:

> I have tried to illustrate the complex interplay in our understandings of parents and education of social reforms, social changes and the social sciences. I have argued that what we know of the relations between parents and education can only be understood through particular perspectives. I have also shown that our know-

ledge developed in a particular way, through the application of the social sciences in a changing policy context ... The social-democratic reformer-researcher partnership also influenced the growth and extent of social and family-life changes and our understandings of them ... These perspectives ...ignored issues of race and gender... Parents and education are ... central issues on the public agenda ...[but]..., will remain partial questions until such time as gender is also included explicitly on the agenda. (1993, pp220-1)

This led me, together with colleagues, to develop a series of research projects to explore the minutiae of the impacts of policy developments on families in particular circumstances. In the first study we explored how families of children in their last year in primary school went about the processes of choosing secondary schools. This policy of parental choice of secondary schools had been revised through the Education Reform Act of 1988 and we were keen to explore its impacts and effects upon working class, poor and particular types of family in London. With Anne West and Jane Ribbens we wrote up our study in a book entitled *Mother's Intuition? Choosing Secondary Schools* (1994). We reached the conclusion that:

This study of choice of secondary schools from both the parents' and children's perspectives has shown how the choice process is largely the responsibility of the mother; it has also shown how the concept of responsibility needs to be further elaborated ... We have revealed that family diversity replicates and is replicated in social and educational diversity. No single lone mother family is exactly the same as another and neither is there clear continuity between traditional two-parent families... Overall, our two studies have provided considerable insight into the processes involved in choosing secondary schools and issues that parents and their children take into account. It is evident that families do not take these issues lightly but invest considerable amounts of time and energy into thinking about education and particular schools. However, we have found it hard to disentangle the ways in which families go about this from the broader ways in which families live their lives and give consideration to living in constrained circumstances ... Diversity and choice in education has indeed created and exacerbated social and family diversity. (1994, p.144-146)

We decided to elaborate upon this study by exploring further complexities in the relations between families and schools, especially in terms of different family involvement in choosing primary and secondary schools. In particular, we wanted to explore the extent of mothers' involvement in early childhood education, compared with their involvement later and that of fathers in diverse family circumstances. We especially wanted to compare and contrast families who sent their children to different types of school, comparing state and private schools in London. Again we found that mothers were pre-eminently responsible for their children's upbringing and education. However, there were also major differences between mothers in different family circumstances and class locations, with fathers from middle class families and with their children in private schools also being heavily involved in the choice processes, if not the day-to-day responsibilities. Mothers and fathers differed considerably in their involvement with homework and particular curriculum subjects as well as out of school activities (1997; 1998; and with West, Edge, Davies and Noden, 1998a, b, and c). Thus we have developed a body of evidence about how parents, both mothers and fathers, get involved in aspects of their children's schooling. These parents are from a diversity of social, economic, cultural and racial or ethnic family backgrounds and family structures, such as single, lone or joint households, and from a variety of school circumstances, from primary and secondary, and state to private schools. The central theme which emerges, however, is that mothers are far more routinely and regularly involved than fathers, and that they are severely constrained from other activities by these obligations.

I have also continued to expand upon the increasingly diverse and complex ways in which family and education are linked, through, on the one hand, considering children's perspectives and understandings about home and school, and especially parental involvement in their education (2000 with Ros Edwards and Pam Alldred). In this study we paid particular attention to the ways in which understandings are influenced by locale and context, and the links between studies at school or at home; and how these may be reflected in our explanations about family and education links. What has also emerged again is the key part played by mothers as reported by their children, in a variety of social class, cultural and family circumstances.

Secondly, together with Stephen Ball and Diane Reay, we have explored how families in different social class and ethnically diverse circumstances go about the processes of choice of higher education, in this case using again Bourdieu's theoretical notions as a perspective on different choices for students in very diverse family circumstances. Again, there are clear differences between students from various social class and ethnic family backgrounds in how they go about the processes of choosing or deciding upon courses and universities. (Ball, Davies, Reay and David, 2000; David, Ball, Davies and Reay, 2003). However, what is significant, from this point of view, is that mothers' support, involvement and encouragement of their children's approaches to developing their choices is reported as a greater influence than fathers or the schools. This is particularly true of working class pupils whose mothers have had no experience of higher education. Again, following from our earlier studies, fathers' involvement is the greater where they have had more experience of higher education and are the more middle class. It is again the working class mothers who bear the burden of involvement in their children's education (David *et al*, 2003).

Studies of social change on mothers and education

The Equal Opportunities Commission commissioned Madeleine Arnot, Gaby Weiner and me to conduct a study of the ways in which policy developments and educational reforms, in particular, had affected gender equality in schools. In our report (1996) we showed how there had been contradictory relations and effects between educational reforms and various forms of gender equality in schools, such as examination successes and achievements, school 'cultures' and LEA and school policies and practices. Given these complex patterns, and in particular the changing gender gap in educational attainments in school-based and public examinations, we set out to explain why these transformations may have taken place. We explored the reasons for what we called the closing of the educational gender gap in *Closing the Gender Gap: Post-war Education and Social Change* (1999, with Madeleine Arnot and

Gaby Weiner) by reference to feminism, family, social and policy changes. In particular, we pointed to massive social transformations in family life, through economic and social changes on an increasingly global scale, over the last fifty years. In particular, changes in family life led to changes in women's lives as housewives and mothers and as workers and professionals in paid employment. Through increasing access to educational opportunities women's family lives had been transformed, exemplified by particular women's lives. However, we also pointed to the continuing restrictions on women's working lives, despite extraordinary educational achievements in the last two decades. Employment and public policies have not mirrored the enormous transformations that have taken place in education and family lives.

Conclusions: developing explanations about change in the family and education
What I have tried to review here is how important the broad changing social and political context has been for developing understandings of the relation between changes in family life, mothers and education. In particular, social movements, and especially the women's movement or feminism, have played a crucial part in enabling new ways of thinking about social transformation, community and active participation. The women's movement was initially important for enabling new political ideas and theories about social change and challenges to traditional family lives. It became increasingly important with respect to more nuanced approaches to family life and education, as feminism slowly entered the academy. As feminism as a perspective gradually gained some acceptance within the academy and as part of the disciplines of the social sciences, new methodological approaches such as critical and personal reflections, biographies and auto/biographies gradually began to be acceptable methodological approaches. By the 1990s, reflexivity had become an acceptable and accepted approach to studies, especially on family life, mothers and education. This was reflected in a developing genre of research and scholarship (Luttrell, 1997, 2003; Kenway et al, 1998). This drew from feminist and other sociological analyses.

For example, such approaches as locating reflections in an auto-biographical vein have become not only accepted but fashionable. Another instance of this may be found in an edited book with Diana Woodward (1998) *Negotiating the Glass Ceiling: Senior Women in the Academic World.* This collection explores personal reflections and explanations of family and education in women's lives through sixteen women's accounts of their lives within the academy. These women are all senior in the academy across two post-war generations; those who were young women at the end of the Second World War and those born in this period. These two generations had contrasting family lives, especially about being mothered and becoming mothers. This illustrates a growing theme in feminist scholarship and pedagogy, and it is that of the role of the academy in women's family lives; from it being influential for women as students from diverse family lives to its role for women as academics and managers in higher education.

Secondly, Ann Curthoys (2000) also explored how generations of feminists over the last thirty years, since the start of second wave feminism, have had to grapple with different issues, challenges and contexts. She too has reflected on her own developments in Australia that map on to my own reflections. As a feminist and a feminist mother, she has remarked upon how cultural, social, economic and political transformations have meant that even personal and private family matters are felt and understood very differently now from thirty years ago. Younger generations of women from a diversity of social, ethnic and cultural family backgrounds have not experienced the same constraints and strictures that the first generation of feminists felt in creating new family lives. They have faced different challenges about how to develop their own social and sexual identities as women as Walkerdine (1997), and with Lucey and Melody (2001) have illustrated for a particular generation of young women.

Thus feminist scholarship, methodologies and pedagogy in the academy have become far more important and complex over the last 30 years since the start of second wave feminism. For me personally, what started as a political interest and concern about topics of mothers and education has now become intertwined with issues about the pedagogy and practices of feminism and feminist methodologies within sociology in the academy. This perspective also now requires critical engagement not only with feminist theories and methodologies but with how these map on to notions of reflection and reflexivity.

Thinking about one's location, personal position and political perspectives, especially on democratic participation and community or family involvement, are vital for feminist approaches. So too is consideration of the wider political and policy context, and how this maps on to and constrains particular changes and developments in family life and their interrelations with education, broadly framed. There is also currently the complex question of how to address and engage critically with the growing political and policy debates especially in England on home school relations or families, particularly mothers and education. Here new concepts of social and emotional capital, drawing on new and complex theoretical developments by political scientists such as Puttnam (2000), sociologists such as Coleman (1997) and by contrast the prolific French theorist Bourdieu, have gained currency and credence in the public and political arenas. However, they tend to ignore or render invisible feminist theorising and gender relations in personal and political life even though they draw implicitly on theories about participation and involvement in community. This is especially the case with Puttnam's notions of social capital relating to civic engagement and political participation.

Just as feminist perspectives on education and family are now intertwined so too are the wider policy contexts, where government in Britain amongst other countries is now developing partnerships between home and school or families and education. Just how do we understand and account for these developments in home-school agreements as families and education are becoming ever more complex? What seems intuitively clear, however, is how much more extensive the responsibilities of motherhood are becoming as motherhood moves from appearing to be an intimate, private and personal responsibility to being performed as a public and profoundly political responsibility at all levels within education, including the academy.

Note

1 This was a modified and revised version of a paper prepared for the edited volume by Sharon Abbey from the plenary presentation to the International Conference on Mothers and Education at Brock University, St Catherine's, Canada, October 1st to 3rd 1999. My inaugural lecture at Keele University on November 22nd 2000 entitled From Keighley to Keele also drew on similar material (David, 2002).

2

Mothers' involvement in their children's schooling: Social Reproduction in action?

Diane Reay

The recent history of parental involvement

Partnership between parents and teachers has become enshrined in educational policy (DES, 1985; 1986; 1988). Parents are increasingly encouraged to become not only consumers within education but also 'active partners in the production of educated children' (McNamara *et al*, 2000: p 474). The 1985 white paper *Better Schools* emphasised the importance of home-school links, arguing that schools could be more effective if they could rely on the co-operation and support of parents in the pursuit of shared objectives, and urged that schools should explain their aims and policies to parents and associate parents with their work. Three years later the 1988 Education Reform Act promised parents much more information, through league tables, about the performance of schools and individual pupils. The Conservative Government's aim with these changes was to produce better educational standards, based on individual parents' demands (David, 1993). Parents were to be encouraged to become consumers within education. A further aspect of this consumer orientation lay in the promotion of parental choice. Parents were to be allowed to choose the best school to suit their children's educational needs. The reality, however, has been somewhat different to the policy rhetoric. Since the inception of the policy there has been a growing body of research which demonstrates that educational markets are class and race-biased (Ball, 2003). Parents are making choices on the basis of the perceived class and, in some instances, racial composition of schools (Reay and Lucey, 2003; Reay, 2004).

The growing consumer-orientated perspective was particularly evident in the 1991 Parent's Charter. Under the Charter parental rights to information about schools and their own children's progress and results in the context of wider performance would be mandatory. Parents' rights to know were to be enlarged through five key documents: a report about each individual child; regular reports on the school from independent inspectors; a performance table for all local schools; a prospectus about individual schools; and an annual report from a school's governors (p 7). In addition the Charter also made clear to parents that they too had responsibilities. By 1991, the whole approach to parent-school relations had shifted from one about how to ensure some measures of equity to how to ensure parental rights and responsibilities in order for individual parents to be able to influence each child's educational success in formal examination situations (David, 1993). Perhaps the best summation of the state-of-play in relation to parental involvement at the beginning of the 1990s was provided by Philip Brown:

> We are entering a 'third wave'......which is neither part of a final drive to 'meritocracy', nor the result of a socialist victory for educational reform. To date, the 'third wave' has been characterised by the rise of the educational parentocracy, where a child's education is increasingly dependent on the wealth and wishes of parents, rather than the ability and efforts of pupils....the ideology of parentocracy involves a major programme of educational privatisation under the slogans of 'parental choice', 'educational standards', and the 'free market'. (1990: 66-7)

Since then there has been an increased emphasis on the accountability of both teachers and parents. During the 1990s parental involvement was officially recognised as a key factor in school improvement and effectiveness (Reynolds and Cuttance, 1992), and in 1994 became a requisite part of a school's development plan (Ofsted, 1994). Ofsted guidelines issued the following year (1995: 98) encouraged inspectors to explore how well schools help parents to understand the curriculum, the teaching it provides and how this can lead to parents and teachers working together to provide support at home.

We have now reached a point when parental involvement is no longer optional. Under the Labour Government, elected in 1997, there has been an intensification of the move from parental rights to increased parental responsibilities initiated under the previous Conservative administration (Whitty *et al*, 1998). Edwards and Warin (1999) go as far as to argue that collaboration between home and school seems to have been superceded by the colonisation of the home by the school. Certainly, schemes like PACT and IMPACT, devised to ensure that parents' support their children's reading and numeracy development, are widespread (Merttens and Vass, 1993), while in 1999 home-school agreements became a statutory requirement, despite considerable disquiet from both educationalists and parent groups. According to the Government White Paper *Excellence in Cities* (DfEE, 1998a):

> All schools should, in discussion with parents develop a home-school contract. These agreements will reflect the respective responsibilities of home and school in raising standards, stating clearly what is expected of the school, of the parent and the pupil.

The home-school agreement policy is an initiative which many educationalists fear will move beyond parental obligations into regulation. As Joan Sallis (1991) argues, the concern is that the emphasis of agreements will shift to lecturing parents on inadequacies they may be unable to remedy, and that those feelings of inadequacy will only be increased. What has become increasingly apparent is that in the 2000s parental involvement has been conscripted by the Government's standards agenda and has become a key means by which schooling can tap into the cultural capital resources of parents in the policy drive to raise educational standards (Brain and Reid, 2003). So how have these changes impacted on the arena of educational equality? The Government's professed goal, like that of its predecessor, is to facilitate merito-cratic processes and moves towards a 'classless' society. However, I want to argue, by drawing on data from two different research projects, that to date all these changes have accomplished little, and in some cases, have damaged, the possibilities of achieving greater equality in education.

The impact of social differences on involvement in schooling

The current enthusiasm for yet more and more parental involve-ment among policy makers has failed to take into account the dangers some kinds of parental involvement pose to pupils' equal opportunities for educational resources. Aspects of parental involvement and schools' accountability to parents may work against equal opportunities. First, parents' personal histories and their educational experiences influence their involvement in their children's schooling, particularly their effectiveness in dealing with teachers. Such differences are rooted in social class, ethnicity and race. Where children's class and cultural background bears little resemblance to that of their teachers, connections between home and school may be minimal and tenuous.

Secondly, the concerns of involved parents are often narrow and aimed primarily at gaining advantage for their own children. While the new century has seen growing levels of anxiety about educa-tional achievement that cross class and race, it is primarily middle class parents who are juggling intense anxieties about their chil-dren's education alongside the pursuit of their educational advan-tage (Jordan, Redley and James, 1994; Ball, 2003). The combina-tion of relative affluence, educational expertise and higher levels of confidence and entitlement in relation to children's schooling give middle class families options most of the working class families do not have. Many middle class families are able to compensate for what they perceive to be gaps in the state provision by employing tutors and attempting to modify the provision the school makes for their child, all the while continuing to complement what the school offers through mothering work in the home. In both the US and the UK there has been a history of middle class parental action directed at controlling both teachers and working class parents (Sieber, 1982; McGrath and Kuriloff, 1999; Jellison Holme, 2002). Currently, middle class parental action in the UK is leading to increasing class and racial segregation both between and within schools, from pressure for streaming on the presumption that their children will be allocated to top sets, to the avoidance of schools with a sizeable cohort of black and/or white working class pupils who might hinder their own child's learning (Bagley, 1996; Butler, 2003).

The differential impact of social class positioning and ethnicity means that parents are dealing with different layers of continuity and discontinuity between their own, and their children's, educational experiences. Where parents are positioned on this continuity/discontinuity spectrum has important consequences for both the quantity and quality of involvement in children's schooling (Vincent, 1997; 2000). Unlike the harmonious, anodyne relationships presented in many of the parental involvement texts, in reality parent-teacher relationships are characterised by a struggle for control and definition. Teachers have two broad sets of relationships to manage: 'with the assertive, demanding middle class parents on the one hand and with the seemingly passive, disengaged working class parents on the other' (Crozier, 2000:123). One consequence is that school-parent links, even in predominantly working class schools, are dominated by middle class parents. Schools tend to offer their scarce resources to those who demand them most vociferously rather than to those in the greatest need. I want to examine these processes more closely by drawing firstly on a case study of mothers' involvement in their children's schooling in two urban primary schools (Reay, 1998), and secondly on data from an ESRC project on the transition to secondary schooling (Reay and Lucey, 2003).

Social Reproduction in action?
The first striking inequality to emerge in the first study was one of gender (Reay, 1998). Within a majority of families there was a clear division of labour in which children's schooling was seen as primarily the mother's responsibility. There was little evidence in any of the women's accounts of men being involved in monitoring or supporting their children's educational performance. Intense

daily work with children was very much the province of the mother. They were the ones with the finger on the pulse. Men occasionally helped out with schoolwork and, particularly in middle-class homes, would find time to attend parents' evenings in school, but what came across very clearly was that parental involvement meant very different things to mothers and fathers. As one father explained when turning down my request to interview him 'Well I suppose I'm typical of most dads in that I'm only involved at a distance'.

However, mothers rarely had the option of being involved 'at a distance'. The research found very little difference among women, regardless of their social class or ethnicity, in either the importance they attached to education or the mental energy they devoted to their children's schooling. Where they did differ was in the level of difficulty they had to negotiate in order to be involved. Mothers' own educational histories continued to exert a powerful influence on their involvement in the present. Many of the working class women had had negative experiences of schooling which undermined any sense of expertise in relation to academic work and left them feeling disempowered in relation to education. They also talked about having mothers who were too busy working a double shift in the home and the labour market to devote any time to their educational progress. In contrast, the middle class mothers were far more likely to refer to positive educational experiences and parental interest in their schooling.

Inequalities resulting from the past were compounded by those in the present. Working class mothers, particularly if they were bringing up children without the financial and emotional support of a partner, were very hard pressed, and talked of how little free time they had after finishing paid work. Cathy's comment below was typical:

> When I get in in the evening the first thing I do is cook them something, get them to eat, a little bit of schoolwork or whatever. You see by the time I pick them up at half five or six o clock it hardly leaves you any time to do the schoolwork. You are kind of thinking about getting them ready for school the next day, you know, making sure they've got clean underwear, something ironed,

sorting out something they may need to take into school the next day. Straight away I need to start thinking about what needs to be done, meals, washing up, cleaning, ironing and on top of that the spellings and the reading – it's hectic.

Despite all the time and energy mothers like Cathy devoted to their children's schooling, they just could not compete with their middle class counterparts. A few of the middle class families I interviewed were spending over £100 a week on private tuition and cultural activities such as music and drama for their child – more than two of the working class lone mothers on benefit were getting in total to live on. However, the norm among the middle class families was to pay for at least one out of school activity, while a sizeable minority paid for their child to attend two or three.

Being able to afford culturally and educationally enriching activities is only one aspect of middle class educational advantage. Many of the middle class parents had themselves done well at school and this educational success translated into self confidence and a sense of entitlement in relation to parental involvement. The middle class mothers were far more adept at getting their viewpoint across in dialogue with teachers when there were any disagreements or tensions between home and school, displaying certainty, self assurance and an ability to counter opposing viewpoints. In contrast, the working class mothers were much more hesitant and apologetic and far more likely to disqualify and, at times, contradict themselves when talking to teachers. They sometimes spoke of coming away from meetings with school staff feeling that they 'hadn't been listened to'. Maggie Maclure and Barbara Walker's research on parents' evenings reported in *Managing Schools Today* (June/July 1999 and in this volume) found similar feelings of not being listened to, in particular among parents who spoke little English. While the middle class mothers in my study (Reay, 1998) could be assertive in interaction with teachers, the working class women's high levels of anxiety occasionally escalated into displays of temper and, as one of them commented forlornly, 'then there's no way you're going to get your point of view across'.

The current political preoccupation with parental involvement in education is underpinned by an assumption that all parents share an identical experience of involvement in their children's schooling. We have a discourse of parenting in which gendered, racialised and classed notions of parent are not acknowledged, rendering inequalities which exist between parents invisible. As I have tried to show, the reality is very different. In my research I employed cultural capital as a conceptual tool for examining how mothers' activities, despite apparent similarities, add up to significant class differences. It was middle-class mothers' combination of relative affluence, educational expertise and 'self-certainty' that gave them options most of the working class mothers did not have. While most mothers conceptualised their relationship to schooling as one of complementing the education their children received, with the working-class mothers talking in terms of 'supporting the school' and 'backing the teacher up' to describe their relationship to schooling, a further group, in particular middle-class mothers, saw their role as a compensatory one. Other mothers, also predominantly middle-class, spoke about their efforts to modify the school provision. These three roles were by no means mutually exclusive. Middle-class mothers moved in and out of different positions with regard to schooling.

It was cultural capital which facilitated this weaving in and out of different roles and provided the middle class mothers with choices that were not open to their working class counterparts. This range of options and the ways in which middle class mothers could draw on them is exemplified in Barbara's account:

> One is the support I give him at home, hearing him read, making him read every night, doing homework with him, trying to get the books he needs for his project. I see that as a support role. The other side, in the particular case of Martin, is where he has had difficulties and finds reading very, very difficult. So a lot of my time has been spent fighting for extra support for him and I mean fighting.

However, later on in the interview she discusses the tuition Martin receives: 'Well he just wasn't making enough progress in school so we decided we'd have to get him a tutor.'

Providing the 'trimmings'

So cultural capital played a crucial role in the extent to which mothers could provide their child with what middle-class Lelia defines as 'the trimmings'. She said 'school is there to take the main responsibility for her learning and we provide the trimmings'. Lelia was able to draw on the cultural capital to weave, seemingly effortlessly, between complementing, compensating for, and modifying her child's school site provision. Naomi had had a Maths tutor for over two years. Lelia's intervention on the school site had resulted in Naomi's inclusion in a gifted writer's group, while Lelia read with Naomi every evening and actively supported the school's curriculum offer in other ways.

Cultural capital is implicated in the ability of mothers to draw on a range of strategies in supporting their children's schooling. Financial resources, confidence in relation to the educational system, educational knowledge and information about schooling all had a bearing on the extent to which mothers felt empowered to intervene in their child's educational trajectory and the confidence with which they embarked on such action. By contrast, for Angie whose account stresses over and over again the importance of education, her personal feelings of incompetence and lack of confidence mitigated against her embarking on any action with a sense of efficacy:

> I have tried, I really have. I knew I should be playing a role in getting Darren to read but I wasn't qualified. Therefore it put extra pressure on me because I was no good at reading myself, it was too important for me to handle and I'd get very upset and angry at Darren.

Attempting to modify the school's offer also had unpredictable and upsetting consequences:

> I always found if I went to the classteacher, she'd take it very personal and think I was attacking her. I wasn't. I was just bringing it to her attention in case she didn't know, you know, that in my opinion he's not progressing. The way I see him and from what I expect of him I don't see the progress. But I'd say 'I'm not saying that it's because you're not teaching my son. I do realise you have a class of thirty and you're only one person and you do so much

and you're expected to do a lot of other things because the National Curriculum expects so much of you. I do understand about that. But what can I do about his reading?' But when I did go to the classteachers I think they took it too personal and felt I was attacking them when really it was that it is so important I couldn't let it go.

It is important to reiterate that there exists a significant minority of parents whose own negative experiences of schooling makes involvement in their children's schooling difficult, even painful (McNamara *et al*, 2000). Working class mothers invariably cited the pitfalls, dangers and misunderstandings they encountered in their own education. Working-class mothers who feel ill-equipped to engage in repair work in the home and lack financial resources are reliant on the school to get the job done. For Josie, in particular, the school had come to be perceived as 'the last and only resort'. Her personal history of immigration, working-class background and academic failure resulted in a sense that there were no other options:

> When I went to see his teacher I was pretty upset about Leigh not reading and it may have come across like 'how come Leigh's not reading. If you aren't hearing him read what are you doing then?'I was maybe coming across like that but what I meant was can he possibly have some extra time. Can someone hear [sic, for God's sake, give him some extra reading and let him get on because it's making my life harder. I was getting so anxious about him not reading cos I couldn't really help him. I'd get upset and frustrated and it wasn't doing Leigh any good because if he can't read what was happening. (Josie Milner)

Josie's words resonate with those of the Latino immigrant parents Ramirez (2003) interviewed in California. Like Josie, they felt that schools did not listen or care to listen to their needs as parents. There is no need for me to explicate the subtext of inequity lurking beneath Josie's words because Josie goes on to provide her own cogent summation of how increasing reliance on parental involvement within the British educational system is perpetuating educational inequalities.

> You need parental involvement. You need parents to be able to complement what you're doing but that's all it should be. It

shouldn't be any more. You see not all people speak English, not all parents read and write so how can they help their children at home. They're at a disadvantage anyway so when they come to school they've got to have the help there. You should just be able to say to the teacher 'Look, I can't do it. You're qualified, can you do something about it?' without the teacher getting all upset about it. There's a lot of parents who can't, just can't do it.

Other mothers also resisted a construction of themselves as their children's teachers. This ambivalence about assuming a teaching role was rooted in mothers' differential access to dominant cultural capital. It was related to a variety of factors; mothers' own negative experiences of schooling, feelings that they lacked educational competences, the refusal of some children to see mothers as educational experts and the amount of time mothers had available to undertake educational work with children.

Repairing children's perceived educational deficits was an easier process if mothers had access to material and cultural resources. Women need to feel confident about tackling educational work in the home and to have access to material resources to support such work. Without these other essential ingredients of cultural capital, I found that the time of mothers like Angie and Josie did not count to anything like the same extent. Yet, it is mothers such as Josie and Angie who are being targeted under current educational initiatives despite the fact that they are the mothers with the least resources with which to meet government demands for parental involvement.

'Protecting our children's interests': middle class mothers making social reproduction work

In the ESRC project on transitions to secondary school (Reay and Lucey 2003) the data reveals the paramount importance for middle class parents of getting their child into the 'right' sort of secondary school, typically one which produces good examination results. The project, which examined 450 inner London children's transitions from primary to secondary schooling, illustrates some of the ways in which parents, and, in particular, middle class mothers, push their children towards high academic performance. This drive towards academic excellence has resulted in increasing numbers of middle-class parents in the inner city, especially those rich in cultural capital but less endowed with economic capital, seeking to bypass what they see as the failings of the state system by entering their children for selective school examinations. Out of our predominantly working class sample of 450, 31 children, 25 of them middle class, took part in selective school examinations. Recent research has revealed how middle class parents are more likely to make the decision about secondary school, sometimes overtly, but more often by guiding the child to make what is seen to be the 'right' decision (Ball, 2003). In contrast, working class parents tend to prioritise the child's preference (Reay and Ball, 1997).

Middle class Sally's first choice is a popular girls' comprehensive which is local to her and where she has many contacts. However, her preference is overruled by her mother, who according to Sally, asked:

> Oh Sally would you mind doing a couple of tests to get into a good secondary school?' and I'm like 'okay but how many is a couple?' and she says 'four' and I'm like 'seriously!'. At first I thought she was joking.

As I have argued in an earlier paper (Reay, 2000) the middle class pursuit of excellence and mothers' efforts to secure middle class social reproduction is not without its costs (see also Lucey and Reay, 2002). One consequence of sacrificing current for future happiness is that there are emotional costs for middle class children and these are evident in Sally's mother's text:

> I think it's taken its toll and I think she's expressing it physically, she's never had so many colds and whatnot as this year. I think she's somatizing actually. But she can't feel that she can go along with all the kids at school who, and her friends who are already at Hamlyn Girls and just be happy, like her best friend is at Hamlyn already, she can't just be happy thinking that she's going to join her, she's got to think that she might go to Longford House. She's in a very difficult position really. As a parent I could say well OK we'll settle for Hamlyn, but I just don't feel, taking a longer view, that I could feel happy with that decision, so I'm prepared to sit with the anxiety of not knowing till the summer.

But there are wider consequences beyond individual repercussions in the growing middle class retreat into 'safe' segregated spaces within the state sector (Butler, 2003). Barbara Ehrenreich (1990), writing about American society, argues that the nervous uphill climb of the professional middle class accelerates the downward spiral of society as a whole: 'towards cruelly widening inequalities, towards heightened estrangement along lines of class and race, and towards the moral anesthesia that estrangement requires. The professional middle class was born with the delusion that it stood outside of the class struggle... Today, it has, in large numbers, joined the problem' (250-1). Ehrenreich's 'moral anesthesia' affects the British middle classes no less than their American counterparts. Within a culture of rampant privatisation and marketisation, middle class strategies of social reproduction in both countries increasingly focus exclusively on the individualistic pursuit of self interest to the exclusion of any notion of the greater social good. And it is important as a feminist educational researcher to recognise that it is women who are mainly responsible for this routine day-to-day work of social reproduction. Only then can we begin to analyse the wider power dynamics that middle class mothers are caught up in just as their working class counterparts.

Conclusion

The research studies of mothers' work in support of children's education within the state system, discussed above, suggest a relationship between women and social class that is quite different from orthodox perspectives which view their activities as largely peripheral. Thirty years ago Basil Bernstein suggested that changes in the composition of the middle classes were transforming the mother 'into a crucial preparing agent of cultural reproduction who provides access to symbolic forms and shapes the dispositions of her children so they are better able to exploit the possibilities of public education' (Bernstein, 1973: 131). The mothers, particularly the middle-class mothers, in both these studies are at the front line of social reproduction, investing heavily in terms of time and mental and emotional labour. Mothers have a different relationship from fathers to the generation of cultural capital and, concomitantly, social class. It is mothers who are making cultural capital work for their children. And it is they, more than men, who appear to be the agents of social class reproduction. In particular, mothering work bridges the gap between family social class and children's performance in the classroom. Maternal practices demonstrate that class is much more than materiality (Reay, 1998). It is played out not only in mothers' activities in support of children's schooling but also in women's attitudes, assumptions and confidences about their children's education.

Class practices are historically specific. At the beginning of the twenty first century class processes within families are integrally linked to the operations of the wider marketplace. An analysis which conceptualises mothering work as strategically located in relation to schooling systems allows for an understanding of mothering work as social reproduction in action. Within a capitalist society in which market forces are ascendent (Jordan, Redley and James, 1994), 'acting in their child's best interests' inevitably means middle class mothers are simultaneously acting against the interests of the children of other, less privileged, mothers. As I have pointed out, this is not to blame middle class mothers but rather to see all mothers as caught up in educational markets which operate on the (il)logic of 'to her who has yet more shall be given'. Educational success becomes a function of social, cultural and material advantages in which mothers' caring within the family is transmuted by the operations of the wider marketplace to serve its competitive, self interested individualistic ethos. Mothers' practical maintenance, educational and emotional work underpins the workings of educational markets contributing to a culture of winners and losers within which one child's academic success is at the expense of other children's failure.

Theorising such social inequalities has become increasingly problematic within a contemporary educational marketplace underpinned by a rhetoric of classlessness. Current discourses of classlessness perpetrate the fantasy that ungendered parents only have to make the right choices for their children for educational success to automatically follow. As the words of the women in both research studies illustrate, the reality is far more complex. It is one in which gender, 'race' and class continue to make significant differences. In Britain class infuses everyday practices and social interactions. As Beck argues: 'It is evident in speech...in the sharp class divisions between residential areas.....in types of education, in clothing and in everything that can be included under the concept of 'lifestyle' (Beck, 1992: 102).

Implicit within the concept of 'a classless society' are more equitable social relations and enhanced mobility. However, despite all the talk of classlessness and increased social mobility, British class differentials in educational attainment remain the same as they were thirty years ago (Bell, 2003). Parental, and in particular, mothers' involvement in children's schooling contributes to the maintenance of this inequitable status quo. This is not the same as asserting that reducing parental involvement will result in the reduction of educational inequalities. Rather, I would argue that within the contemporary individualistic, competitive, educational marketplace with its rhetoric of 'doing the best for your own child', the middle classes will always utilise their economic and cultural resources to ensure the continued reproduction of their children's educational advantage.

3

Beyond the Call of Duty: the impact of racism on black parents' involvement in their children's education

Gill Crozier

Introduction

The long awaited expression of concern over the under-achievement of black and Asian children witnessed over the past 12 months or so has resulted in the call for a Committee of Enquiry (Black Underachievement Conference, the Greater London Authority, March 2002); the production of DfES guidance (2003) on how to address black underachievement and the setting up of a resource network by the Teacher Training Agency (TTA) (www.multiverse.ac.uk). These developments signify an engagement or re-engagement with these issues. There have been a number of events, in many cases tragic, and conferences such as the one just referred to that have contributed to this 'awakening'.

There are however a set of concerns that have arisen from these conferences and debates. There seems for example to be disregard for the research that has been carried out into black children's underachievement by for example Gillborn and Youdell (2000),

Gillborn (1995), Mac an Ghaill (1988), Wright (1992), Blair and Bourne (2000). Consequently even though this research identifies a number of reasons for this underachievement, the discussion flails around looking for someone or something to blame. This is usually the children themselves or the parents.

At the GLA conference some identified the target as black parents. According to a *Times Educational Supplement* article reporting on the conference entitled, 'Get Involved, head tells black parents' (Bloom 15 March, 2002), William Atkinson, head of a London School, said that lack of involvement by black parents in school life was often to blame for their children's academic problems. 'Parents should stop blaming schools and start taking responsibility for their children's progress.' Moreover, he said, 'Part of the problem is the children do not belong to a culture that supports success.'

At a one day conference in Derby (2002) organised by The 1990 Trust which looked at black children's underachievement, Tony Sewell also criticised black parents for not taking greater responsibility for their children: 'for letting go too soon.' In an article in the *Times Educational Supplement* on 29 March, Atam Vetta (2002) added his contribution to laying the blame at parents' door, arguing that parents of African Caribbean origin and also of Pakistani and Bangladeshi origins are probably to blame for their children's underachievement because they most likely have no family members who have ever been to University. These criticisms are over simplistic and ignore the impact and complexity of race and class and gender dynamics. Moreover their unsubstantiated accusations are not just against black parents but in the main against black mothers.

This chapter presents a very different view of black parents'/mothers' involvement. It demonstrates the extent of parental involvement and the difficulties parents and children face in spite of this investment. The involvement of the parents in trying to achieve for their children a fair, more positive and successful educational experience is extensive.

The chapter describes the deep concerns that the parents hold about their children's education. As one mother put it: '...they're being attacked right, left and centre.... like there's a war against them.' They recount unfair practices being meted out to their children, experiences of exclusion, which in some instances were found to be totally unwarranted, and tell how they themselves have been ignored by teachers when they tried to get the school to address their children's needs. However, my main purpose is concerned less with the underachievement of black children in itself, although inherently connected with this; it is primarily concerned with the emotional labour, domestic labour (providing meals, the school uniform, resources; ensuring the child gets to school on time) and what I have termed, professional labour (labour expended in supporting the homework, listening to the reading; providing educational experiences out of the home – the work of the teacher) that parents undertake in the support, defence and protection of their children in the face of a system that is failing to meet their children's needs.

The Research Study

The chapter draws on semi and unstructured interviews with 32 parents: 27 mothers and five fathers, based in two cities in the south west of England (cities A and B). Twenty five of the parents were interviewed over the past two years and seven of the parents were interviewed seven years ago (see also Crozier, 1996). Parents were asked about their views on their children's education and their own role within this. Three couples were interviewed and two group interviews (four in one group and three in the other) were carried out. Twelve mothers and one father were lone parents, although in the case of the father the mother took major responsibility for the child. In four cases family structure was unknown. The remaining 15 were either married or in a partnership. The interviews were taped and transcribed and analysed using a grounded theory approach (Strauss and Corbin, 1990). The parents are mainly of African Caribbean origin, although one lone mother is of Pakistani origin, is a Christian and has mixed race children, and one mother is of Indian origin. Three of the African Caribbean mothers had white partners; one of the mothers is white and married to a Jamaican. One of the fathers is of Nigerian origin. Parents' social class locations ranged from professional to unskilled and unemployed. Half of the parents had either returned to further study for a degree, a diploma or a professional qualification or were intending to do so, having left school at 16 with few qualifications. Nine of the parents had three or more children; of these two had four, one had five and one had six. Five parents had one and the rest had two. Parents who had more than one child often had difficult situations, in relation to school, to deal with for all or several of their children.

Parental Involvement as Emotional Work

What do I mean by 'emotional work'? In talking about parental involvement as emotional work I am conflating the concept of 'emotional labour' written about by others such as Nicky James (1989) and Arlie Hochschild (1983) and the emotional expenditure involved in emotion work. This latter idea might be nearer Diane Reay's (2000) concept of 'emotional capital'. James defines emotional labour as: 'a social process in which labour is employed in dealing with others' emotions' (James, 1989 p21) and according to Hochschild it is the 'the management of feeling to create a publicly observable facial and bodily display'. 'Emotional labour', she goes on to say, 'is sold for a wage and therefore has exchange value' (Hochschild, 1983 p7). But Hochschild also uses the term synonymously with emotion work and emotion management to refer to the same acts done in a private context where they have use value (*ibid*) . Diane Reay talks of emotional capital as '... not coterminous with emotional involvement but ... can be understood as the emotional resources passed on from mother to child through processes of parental involvement' (p569).

Here I am concerned with the emotional expenditure that mothers and to some extent fathers invest as a result of the pressure the children and de facto the parents themselves are under in the educational setting. I am using the concept of emotional work to add to an understanding of the kind of investment parents place in their children's education in addition to the already understood if not always recognised domestic and 'professional' labour. In addition to parents' emotional expenditure, drawing on Nicky James' and Diane Reay's work, I also begin to explore the use of emotional work in the shoring-up of children's own emotions and self-confidence in the face of a series of negative experiences that they endure as part of their schooling.

In employing the concept of emotional work I am seeking to present these experiences and explain their implications for the parents. In addition, I seek to challenge the continued over-simplification of parental involvement discourses that characterise involved parents as equalling successfully achieving children and uninvolved parents as equalling unsuccessful children; in turn this challenge muddies the water regarding 'acceptable' involvement which, I have argued elsewhere, is based on a passive acceptance of the status quo (Crozier, 2000). The parents here by contrast are engaged in resisting discriminatory practices and thus defending their children, rescuing their children and comforting them in the face of abuse and humiliation. As Nicky James and Arlie Hochschild have said, emotional labour is frequently invisible and therefore is not recognised as 'labour' at all. Moreover, the significance of this work is not recognised either. This is clearly exemplified by the recent attacks on black parents, referred to earlier.

Diane Reay argues that emotional capital is less closely associated with social class differences than for example Bourdieu's concept of cultural capital. However, she does say that 'poverty is not normally an environment in which emotional capital can normally thrive' (2000, p581). The parents in my study cut across the range of social classes, educational knowledge and qualifications and also incomes. However, they all described an engagement with their children's education comparable to the interventionist orientation undertaken by white middle class parents in the drive to enable their children to achieve academically (Crozier, 2000, Reay, 2000, Reay, 1998).

I turn now to an analysis of the empirical data which illustrate the nature of the emotional work carried out by the parents. The emotional work of course cannot be detached from the domestic labour or the 'professional labour' involved in parental involvement. Parents' emotional labour as manifested in the research can be structured around several themes: Concern about racism; Compensating for school failure; Managing feeling; Being ignored and Being humiliated.

Concern about racism: 'exit' and 'choice'

The emotional labour and resulting anxiety about schooling often began before the children got to school or at the transitional stage between primary and secondary school. The parents were aware from their experience as children or that of their siblings that racism could be an issue. They were also aware of more recent reports about academic underachievement of black children and the disproportionate exclusion rates amongst this group.

The black parents expressed anxiety regarding the treatment of their primary school aged children. They were not confident that teachers had the ability or willingness to deal with the issues their children might face. Consequently they were anxious about what was going to happen to their children on going to school and particularly secondary school. This led many respondents to take or try to take pre-emptive action by seeking out a school which they thought would best serve their child's needs and eschew racist practices. Most of the parents lived in the inner city where most minority ethnic groups lived. Many of the parents associated the large numbers of black children in the inner city schools with a poor quality educational experience and consequently did not want to send their children there. This could be seen as what Reay and Lucey (2003) have referred to as self-demonisation. However, the parents are not blaming the (black) children themselves but rather juxtaposing large numbers of black children with teachers' inability to relate to, and meet the needs of these children. Also, as Irvine (1990) found in the USA, African Americans believe that resources and quality follow white students (reported in Ladson Billings, 1994 p5). Amongst the parents in this study there was also a recognition that certain predominantly white schools have better exam results (see for example Thrupp, 2000).

Parents therefore either sent their children to primary schools outside the area and in a predominantly white part of the city which required travelling long distances or, where this was not possible, they sought out the most 'reputable' local primary school. Five parents chose private schools for at least part of their child's education. With regard to secondary school those who did not wish to send their children to a private school or could not afford it (only three were able to do this for *all* of their child's education and two of these only through the Assisted Places Scheme which was then abolished in 1998) tried to get their children into one of the two grammar schools in City A, a CTC in city A, a foundation school (formerly grant maintained) in city B or a Church of England School in City A which had a 'good' academic reputation.

Jan and her partner sent their youngest son to a private school at first and justified it in these terms:

> I mean like all parents we want the best for our children and I stayed at home with my son until he was three and a half and [then] looked at different nurseries ... and then we put him in a private school ... the reason we chose that was the fact that ... I suppose partly because I had him at home and he had a one on one with me and we done lots of things and you know like all children he was very bright, he is very bright and I wanted him to be in a class where he was going to get the attention, the class size was going to be small. So that was ... our overriding decision about choosing the school that [he went] to and he started off okay. (Jan, African/African Caribbean; 4/2/01; Occupation un-known; Access course and BSc Business Management)

Another mother (Doris) who had sent her older daughter to a private prep school was clear that because they paid for their daughter's education it was more likely that she would be shielded from racism and discrimination:

> I know that with issues like [racism] they do [the private school] handle it very quickly and very positively. And I think it's because you're paying for it and it's a horrible thing to say but I think the sheer fact that parents are paying for their child's education means that they have more status and power within the school to affect the way that teaching and the social... the way the school is organised socially. (Doris, African Caribbean; part-time university lecturer. 1/8/00; mixed race children)

In order to find the 'best' school from their perspective, parents consulted league tables, information distributed by the schools, or through grapevine knowledge (Ball and Vincent, 1998). Several parents had to go to appeal and lobbied hard to win their desired choice of school. Although other studies have shown that 'active choosers' (Gewirtz *et al*, 1995) and proactively involved parents (Crozier, 2000) tend to be middle class, the difference between the working class parents here and the white working class parents in my other study (Crozier, 2000) with respect to their ability to act in this way, is in relation to the social capital that many of the parents had, particularly through their own experiences of having returned to study at university or FE level and in some cases through their community activism. I would also speculate that their ability to activate and utilise this social capital came to some extent from their 'race' politics and awareness and experience of related struggle. A similar point is made by Hill Collins (1998) in discussing black women's activism in the USA:

> [Black women] working for social justice for particular loved ones often stimulated a heightened consciousness about the effects of institutionalised racism on African Americans as a group. (p28)

In spite of these efforts most of the parents were dissatisfied with their children's experiences. Low expectations by teachers of the children was repeatedly referred to by the parents as a particular source of anxiety and something that they as parents had to address. In some cases this would also give grounds for seeking out an alternative school.

> When my eldest daughter went to school at five she knew every-thing that the teacher was teaching them... they were surprised that she knew all that she knew and I felt that they could have done a lot more to push her along really...She used to come home and complain that that her children were messing about and she couldn't get on so I moved her to a more affluent school...(Shakira, African Caribbean, supply teacher 4/2/01)

Even though Jan and her partner had tried to buy a 'better' experience for their son, it had not proved to be what they expected, as she explained:

> I then didn't feel I could leave my child there on a morning and be confident he was going to be treated fairly and equally with other children and I've noticed some things when I've gone to pick him up from after school that I'd seen happening with a couple of other younger black children now I was not at all happy with and I thought he doesn't have to be here. Well I was very sad about that ...

And so having made the effort to seek out a school, or pay to have some control over the child's educational experience, parents often suffer the disappointment and hurt of betrayal and rejection.

And although Doris and her (white) partner (occupation unknown) had paid to give their daughter a 'good start' they could not continue to pay for her education. They were worried how she would fare in the state system where, they perceived, they would have less influence over the teachers' practices and expectations:

> I am very worried about how [she] will manage in the state system ... I think she is more likely to experience, not full-on racism from the staff. I think it will probably be more subliminal than you know that the sort of direct ... or from her own peer group...

Other parents said that they were 'fed up' with the state system and they would have sent their children to private schools if they could have afforded it, whilst some mothers said that what they really needed was 'black run' or 'black only' schools.

As Aisha explained:

> ...we live in a society where, you know, it's inherently racist and I feel it impacts on us as black people, our perception, where we're at, and it impacts on white people, on white children, black children, ...white teachers, black teachers; it impacts on all of us... And I think that the teachers' perceptions of my son because he had locks on his head – that was very critical...is that he wasn't going to do nothing or go nowhere... . It depends on the teacher and the teacher's perception and on how the teacher's willing to work with him and see him...which is [why] if I had a choice I would put him in a black only school... (Aisha, African Caribbean; diploma in social work; worked with the homeless 3/2/01)

For these parents this was not a possibility as there was no longer a supplementary school in the city.

Compensating for School Failure

In addition to trying to seek out the best school experience for their children wherever they might find this, black parents are frequently faced with the need to make up for the deficiencies of the school system as best they can.

In a sense it could be argued, parental involvement as professional labour such as help with homework or homework monitoring, listening to the child read, providing ICT resources to support homework and course work tasks, could be seen as compensating for the school's inadequacy. The parents in this study had to undertake compensatory measures beyond these rudimentary forms when they saw that the school would not respond to their requests or concerns about their children's progress or needs. In so doing they expended a combination of domestic, professional and emotional labour.

Mrs Banks (Black British; nurse. 6/10/01), for example, had lost faith in the teachers; she felt that they were not supporting her son in his maths and even though he was making good progress in mathematics they refused to put him in a higher set. At first she paid for private tuition in maths (and also in English) but then decided that she too would go back to study GCSE maths so that she could help her son. She and her son went to evening classes to study it together and he took his maths GCSE and passed it a year early.

Shakira discovered that her daughter was not getting homework even though her exams were approaching so went and bought books for her to revise. Some parents though did not have the resources to give extra support. Nina (Black British; social worker. 1/8/00) knew her son was not doing as well as he should and tried repeatedly to lobby the school to give him extra support, which never materialised.

Parents' efforts it seemed were frequently at odds with the practices of teachers' who, according to the parents, were too complacent. The parents felt their efforts at trying to raise their children's aspirations and motivation were undermined by the power and influence of the school. Nina, for instance, described how her son needed to be pushed but the teachers weren't doing so. They were too easily satisfied with his limited, in her opinion, efforts, whereas she wanted him to achieve much more. Yet she felt they had much more influence over him with respect to education. This in turn had consequences for her: 'It's quite upsetting; it can be quite emotional ... because I want my son, you know, I want him to do well and achieve … ' And yet the parents often felt that the pressure they put on their children might be unreasonable. This dissonance between themselves and the school and the potential consequences for the children gave rise to 'see-saw' like responses of not being sure whether they had done enough or too much. This often made the parent feel guilty:

> …it's not everyday I get to do maths … every day she reads but it's not every day I get to do [maths] so that's why I get my guilt trips as well. I think 'oh I should be doing it every day' …. some days she comes in and she's tired and I'm tired as well …and by the time we've turned round and we've eaten and all the rest of it… (Nina, African Caribbean; social worker. August 2000)

One of the most extreme examples of parents compensating for the failure of the school is with regard to exclusion. Some of the parents in the sample had more than one child who had been excluded on one or more occasion. Also there are different types of exclusion. Mr and Mrs Kerr's (white father retired due to ill health; mother Black British; social worker. 1/7/01) daughter Sarah was excluded from school visits because of her alleged poor behaviour. Consequently her parents made up for this by taking her on outings themselves and to 'things like the Tate Gallery…go to exhibitions around here … take her to multicultural events, black history events, all sorts of different things…'. Things they said they would do anyway but they had to ensure that this role was fulfilled because the school had failed to undertake it. As they pointed, out not all parents would have had the resources, cultural or financial, to do this.

Exclusion from school made different kinds of demands on parents. Frequently parents reported that they had no forewarning that there was a problem and they would just get a phone call at work to say their child was being sent home. The added stress involved in this was caused by trying to manage their job and get home to see to their child. Shakira, whose son had been, wrongly as it turned out, excluded from school, gave up her job to look after him at home until he was reinstated in school, which led to financial hardship. Most of the parents reported that their children received barely a few hours a week home tuition or none at all, and no homework was sent home. One mother said she had to 'cut back' to pay for a tutor but could only afford this once a week. Others talked of having to buy the required books that the child would normally have at school.

The exclusion in effect acts like a punishment of not only the child but also the parent. The responsibility for the child's poor behaviour is blamed on the parent/s and so the child is returned to the parent to deal with it. But there seems to be no or little dialogue about what led to the misbehaviour (see also Gillborn and Youdell, 2000). When parents probed to find the cause of exclusion, some found that the punishment was unjust. The consequences of the exclusion for the parents in financial, physical and emotional terms are extensive. In addition to having to ensure the safety and care of their child during the day and trying to provide an education for her/him, there is also the degradation and loss of respect for both child and parent. Where the punishment is unjust, the impact of all of these experiences is even greater.

Managing feeling

The case of Sarah, who had been banned from school trips, provides an example of this. Although banned from school visits, there was one occasion when she was allowed to go on a visit to a themed museum park. During the visit there was some trouble and the school was subsequently banned from the museum. Sarah was blamed. Mr and Mrs Kerr explained how they were shocked and appalled that Sarah had caused all this trouble. They were going to go to the museum to apologise in person but the school stopped them from doing so. Instead they wrote to the museum and wrote to the school to apologise and told them about the positive things that Sarah can and does do. They explained that they didn't want them to think that they were 'bad' parents. As they said: 'We really didn't want them to feel that she just wasn't being raised [properly] or anything because we almost felt 'oh it appears like you know, they don't know how to raise their children'.' As it transpired it wasn't just Sarah but a whole group of children who had been misbehaving.

In these circumstances the parents are having to retrieve the situation for their child; deal with the putative misbehaviour whilst at the same time ameliorating the impact of negativity on the child's self concept. In addition the parents are having to defend their own dignity and integrity as parents. Where the child and *de facto* the parents have been wrongly accused, the parents felt they had been misled by the school which in turn for them demonstrated a lack of respect.

Jan talked about how she tried to support her son by changing the teacher's view of him through her own actions; how she thought it was important to fit in and conform so that her child would be treated fairly, although it was to no avail:

> I was working, then doing uni part time, and on days that I didn't have lectures I'd go in on a morning and help over the lunchtime, and help at playtime or go to the class and help with reading or other things and build a relationship with the teacher, you know, just so that the she could see my son in a different light, but that didn't work.

Many of the parents talked about having to protect their children in similar ways, providing them with 'emotional support'. Ms Banks for example, who described her secondary aged son as having lost all trust in the teachers, explained that her son encouraged her to go into the school to help out in order to 'chaperone him' to monitor what the teachers did which even she thought was an unusual request for a teenager but which showed her the extent of his concerns.

Once again the mothers, in particular, talked about power of the school and the power of the teachers in deciding their children's fate or, as Ms Banks put it, '...at the end of the day they are in control of our children to a point and they can make or break them...'

As well as shielding their children, the mothers tried to inculcate their own emotional capital, as Diane Reay (2000) has described, into their children to give them the strength to continue to strive for academic success. However, the emotional cost began to take its toll for some and optimism began to wane. In the words of Ms Breeze (African Caribbean mother, community care worker) when asked what she hoped for the future for her son: 'I'm struggling, I'm really struggling now.'

Whilst the social situation in the USA may be more extreme for black children (see Hill Collins, 2000; Ladson-Billings, 1994) it is also the case that in Britain children of African Caribbean origin, and especially boys, are more likely to underachieve in school, more likely to be excluded from school, more likely to be un-employed on leaving school and more likely to end up in prison than young people from any other ethnic group. Consequently as Hill Collins (2000) also points out, protecting their children remains a primary concern of black mothers.

Most of the parents in the study had to struggle for their children in some way. For some it was to get the school of their choice; for others it was to obtain more information about their children's academic progress; for others again it was a fight for justice for their excluded child or just better treatment in the school or class-room. As James (1989) also observes, emotional labour is hard work. Hill Collins (2000) found, in the US, that lack of expert knowledge compounded by time pressures and the impact of powerful others results in black mothers having to mother under intolerable conditions.

Being ignored and being humiliated: invisibility and public scrutiny – different sides to the same coin

For many of the parents in this study, the impact of their involve-ment had intolerable consequences. They reported that in spite of their concern, interest, and general involvement, they were not kept informed by the schools. Had they been, they said they could have supported their children and rectified the situation. Shakira for example said that when her eldest daughter was doing her A levels she dropped out, but that no one from the school rang her to tell her that her daughter wasn't going to school. Shakira found this extremely upsetting. Other parents said that they asked for information but weren't given it. In some cases schools were taking initiatives with the children but not informing the parents. Mr and Mrs Kerr for example found out by chance that the school had asked a child psychologist to see Sarah but had never told them.

In their efforts to get information parents were often seen as pushy by the school or were treated with disdain. Some parents also described being treated as a child themselves: 'Sometimes when I go to the school and they're talking to you, I feel intimidated because the way they talk to you sometimes, you feel as if you're the kid...' (Ms Banks). And Mrs Kerr explained that the teachers found her and her husband challenging because they questioned the teachers' or school's practice. She said: 'In fact [Sarah's] head of year Mr [A], he actually said,... he said that he found me quite challenging which I thought was a bit... He's treating me a bit like he treats [Sarah]; he finds [Sarah] challenging.'

Infantalising others provides a justification for ignoring and marginalising them, given the position of children in this society. It also obfuscates black parents and particularly mothers' (given their more active educational role) right to a voice.

Black people are not only silenced in this way but are traditionally put under surveillance and this is a form of control (Gilkes, 1983). Naming and shaming is one manifestation of this kind of surveillance-control strategy and was experienced by Ms Banks. Ms Banks and her partner took their children on holiday which over ran the school holidays by a few days. Ms Banks acknowledged that she had failed to ask the school's permission for this absence but sent a note with her son to the school on the day he returned. When she herself returned to work she discovered that the Education Welfare Officer had telephoned her place of work and told them that her son was missing from school. She returned to work to ridicule from her colleagues, who greeted her with:'Oh, you've been a naughty girl, haven't you?'

Here there are two aspects to the surveillance, the Education Welfare Officer (EWO) and the work colleagues. Not only is Ms Banks a 'naughty girl', infantilised in this instance by her colleagues, but she is also an irresponsible parent demonstrated by the pursuit of the EWO for behaviour which, in line with the recent Antisocial Behaviour Act, will not be tolerated and could lead to on the spot fines (Ward, 2003).

Aisha recounts an incident involving her oldest son.When the police brought him to her place of work in a police car, she, like her son, was humiliated in front of her colleagues. There is the added dimension here of being shown up as not only a 'poor' parent but one whose influence has apparently led to criminality (see Crozier, 2003).

One of the most significant issues about this event is what Aisha herself identifies, that the school called the white parents involved to arrange an appointment, treating them like adults and responsible parents:

> ...[It was the school's] responsibility to let me know what was going on as well. You see what I'm saying, and the school knew he was taken from the premises and brought here but it was all this stuff and ...

> What was interesting is that the boy who actually stole the bike, when they went down and asked about his statement, they phoned his parents. His parents were very middle class [and white]. Phoned his parents and made an appointment with the parents; whether it was convenient for the parents to bring their boy down to talk about what had happened. You see what I'm saying ? And he was the actual perpetrator.

This experience is echoed by Hill Collins when she argues that black women 'who break silence' (and Aisha, as she had said, was seen as troublesome by the school because she did try to 'stand up' for her children) can be silenced and rendered invisible on the one hand and vilified on the other (Hill Collins, 1998 p41).

Conclusion

I have shown that black parents, and particularly mothers, have invested considerable emotional labour, along with domestic and 'professional' labour in their children's education. This has taken the form of trying to ensure their needs are met, compensating for the inadequacies of the education system and protecting or rescuing their children from a negative or educationally damning and damaging experience.

In doing so the parents are taking a stand against a system that pathologises their children and has them marked out as failures, by remaining adamant that their children will succeed academically and in terms of their future careers.

Nicky James (1989) observed that by undertaking the management of feeling and thus regulating emotional expression and protecting others from the demands of emotion, women are acting 'as society's emotional sponges' (p24) . Oakley (1974) also argued that women's role is to deal with tensions that arise from certain emotional expressions and ensure harmonious relationships. In a sense this is exactly what the school is expecting from the parents/ mothers when they exclude the child.

However, although these mothers may soak up the emotions of others they are not passive reproducers of the *status quo*. Rather it has been shown that they invest their own emotional labour into challenging the exclusion decisions, the discrimination, or whatever injustice their child has experienced, in order to achieve something better for her/him – and indeed for other black children.

My account here barely does justice to the extensive engagement in their children's education that the parents entered into. They are motivated not only by their strong commitment to education and wanting their children to do well but also by the impact of institutional racism and the need to defend, rescue and protect their children. Many of these parents had more than one child for whom they had to act in these ways. Enduring endless criticisms of your child as 'bad', rude, troublesome, or seeing your child rejected by the school, is an emotional trial. Emotional work involves the emotions and thus their management, of the 'worker' and those of the person (the children in these cases) who is the object of the emotional work (Sharma and Black, 2001). But of course the role of the parent is much more than managing emotions, as Mrs Kerr reported. When she had to go to the school and hear the complaints and criticisms about one of her children, she turned to the head teacher and said, '... you know it's very hard for me to sit back and hear you talking about [my] child like that because despite what you think he's still our child and we still have to come, and love him and support him...'

Acknowledgements
I am very grateful to Jason Pegg who carried out half of the interviews with the parents in these two studies and also to the parents who gave up so much of their valuable time.

SECTION 2
Participatory Democracy
'no one said it would be easy'

4

Negotiating Public and Private: maternal mediations of home-school boundaries

Jane Ribbens McCarthy with Sue Kirkpatrick

Mediating a child's educational experiences between home and school is one form of participation that a child's primary carer inevitably faces. This generally applies to mothers – fathers are much more likely to have a choice about whether or not to participate in their child's schooling (McKie *et al.*, 2002). Among mothers, the nature and extent of such mediation varies considerably between different individuals, social groups and local and national contexts, and will also be influenced by the ages and active agency of the child/ren themselves (Edwards and Alldred, 2000; Edwards, 2002). But, at the very least, in the compulsory education systems of Western societies, mothers are expected to ensure that their children arrive at school at the required times and with the required personal presentation and equipment. Yet such participation may be quite taken-for-granted by both policy makers and researchers. This taken-for-grantedness may result – at least partly – from the predominance of public agenda and perspectives which makes it difficult to notice the implications for privately based family lives.

In this chapter, I[1] consider the concepts of public and private as these have been used in academic debate. I explore how far these theoretical concepts help to illuminate the lives of mothers in the context of home-school relations. Drawing on some empirically grounded material, I show how these issues may be experienced in the daily lives of mothers. In particular, I explore whether there is any scope for mothers to build on their privately based experiences to resist dominant public discourses and organisational imperatives around the schooling of their children. In this discussion I give explicit attention to the home side of the boundary rather than how it looks from the school side.

Public, private and personal

I was first introduced to the concepts of public and private by Leonore Davidoff at Essex University (see, for example, Davidoff *et al*, 1976 and Davidoff, 1990). Since my concern in my own doctoral work was to help make women's domestically based lives more visible altogether within sociology, these concepts seemed to hold great potential. This enthusiasm was shared with Rosalind Edwards when we were both doctoral students at South Bank University, where she was researching the experiences of women mature students' experiences of moving between home and educational systems (Edwards, 1993a). Over time, we have written several pieces, together and separately, about why we think these concepts are important and what we find significant about their meanings (Edwards, 1993a; Ribbens, 1994; Bell and Ribbens, 1994; Ribbens and Edwards, 1995; Edwards and Ribbens, 1998, Ribbens McCarthy and Edwards, 2001, Ribbens McCarthy and Edwards, 2002).

Throughout these writings, our concerns have centred on the possibilities and ramifications that the concepts of public and private have, firstly for people's understandings of their everyday experiences and, secondly, for the conceptual frameworks that we use as sociologists in writing about people's lives. In doing so, we have been able to draw on extensive and established feminist discussions, that both seek to understand and at times challenge the concepts of public and private. One particularly relevant feature of this feminist work has been to draw attention to the significance of women's/mothers' ways of knowing, and the sorts of knowledge that result, rooted within the concrete details of everyday domestically-based lives (Belenky *et al*, 1986; Smith, 1987; Apthekar, 1989; Edwards, 1993b, Edwards and Ribbens, 1998).

However, the concepts of public and private have also been widely used within other literatures for different purposes, with the potential for much confusion about what is understood by the academic use of these terms. Between these various versions, it is only too easy for some perspectives to be lost and/or misunderstood. Rather than attempting to pin down the concepts in any essentialist – or even definitive – way, Ros Edwards and I have therefore sought instead to make a clear statement about what we think is important about the terms as we understand them, and why we think the (feminist) sociological enterprise needs to maintain this perspective. In the discussion that follows I draw heavily on our most recent writings together on these issues (Ribbens McCarthy and Edwards, 2001; Ribbens McCarthy and Edwards, 2002), where we also lay out in more detail the context and caveats for our arguments.

An overarching theme in our argument concerns the significance of variable understandings of what it means to be an individual. A wide variety of writers in recent years have shown increasing recognition of the historical and cultural specificity of understandings of individuality. Some have discussed how the notion of the autonomous self-directing subject is rooted within post-Enlightenment Western cultures, arising predominantly from the particular experiences of white, middle class men. Others, including key feminist writers, have discussed other versions of individuality, that invoke a more relational or connected sense of self, in which personhood is understood to be integrally bound up with others.

In contemporary Western societies, there is diminishing social space in which people may experience the more relational or connected sense of self, a sense of self that is increasingly marginalised from public social settings and discourse. It is in the context of socially constructed understandings of childhood that we find the primary site for this more connected sense of personhood. This is because childhood has been increasingly elaborated and identified as different from adulthood (Ribbens McCarthy and Edwards, 2000), heavily underpinned by institutional and legislative frameworks. And, since mothers are still overwhelmingly the primary carers of children, the more relational, connected sense of self is likely to be more familiar to women than men.

Further, the lives of mothers and children are not based solely in the home or household, but also occur in various social settings that are seen as appropriate places to take children (Bell and Ribbens, 1994; McKie et al, 2002). Consequently, this connected sense of individuality experienced particularly around childhood is related to, and shared within, child-centred social networks. These then provide social spaces for extensive and elaborate differences in ways of being that can be theorised as a distinction between public and private.

In my discussion here I am following the general practice of discussing the concepts of public and private in dichotomous terms[2], as mutually exclusive and mutually constructed. If we approach public and private in this way, there are some key 'ideal typical' tensions that can be highlighted by these concepts, in terms of:

• understandings of individuality as autonomous or connected (as discussed above)

• an instrumental means-end orientation or an orientation to concrete everyday processes and relationships as important in themselves

• formal (bureaucratic) regulation or informal fluidity

• contractually-governed, universalistic relationships *or* normatively-governed, particularistic relationships (Ribbens McCarthy and Edwards, 2000: 773).

Such variable tensions between different social practices and orientations may be overlaid within different social settings, thus constituting distinct and extensive ways of being, which can be identified by the terms 'public' (to refer the first set of understandings in each case), and 'private' (to refer to the second set of understandings). It is these distinctions around different ways of being for which Ros Edwards and I have been concerned to keep open a conceptual and theoretical space, in order to maintain the opportunity to explore, and make visible, different ways of being between public and private as social settings and associated social practices

Home school boundaries

How does this discussion of public and private relate to the concrete geographical sites of home and school? I first consider how far these are to be understood as discrete and bounded social spaces, and then how far they may also be distinguished by differences in social practices and orientations.

In looking at unfamiliar societies, anthropologists want to determine how they can identify different social settings, and how they are demarcated. They might look, for example, at differences of dress, speech or ritual, as well as the layout of physical space, to identify how people themselves differentiate social settings. The boundary between home and school may be obvious in a physical sense, signalled by the presence of groups of mothers standing by the school gate, but it may also be seen, for example, when a child goes home from school and strips off her school uniform before going out to play, the change of clothing signalling how she has crossed the boundary from formal schooling to informal play.

While boundaries may be outwardly manifested by such symbolic differences as dress or speech, they may also hold significant implications in relation to such matters as people's sense of identity, of where they see themselves as fitting in the world. There may also be implications for people's styles of interaction, in the terms in which Edwards and I have discussed different 'ways of being' between public and private. Particularly significant in the context of home and school may be differences in terms of what sort of knowledge about children is regarded as valid in different settings, or what sort of values are regarded as important.

Anthropologist Sandra Wallman (1978) suggests that social boundaries are likely to be areas of ambiguity, tension and danger because different social settings may carry profoundly different implications. She also suggests that boundaries have two sides to them, and have to be understood from the point of view of people on both sides. What is more, a social setting that has clear boundaries may provide a basis for the exercise of some power and authority *within* that setting. Boundaries between settings are thus also likely to raise issues about power *between* people on each side of the boundary. Indeed, some discussions about school management that use a notion of boundaries explicitly refer to parents as part of the external environment that a school may be seeking to manage.

I would argue that homes and schools are indeed quite different sorts of social settings. On the one hand, schools are formal, bureaucratically-bound organisations, operating in a context of public policies and imperatives. Schools have to take an overview of all children in their remit, balancing out the needs of one child against the need to co-ordinate the school as an organisation. Berry Mayall (1994) points out that the coercive framework of the school involves a different sort of authority that is sharply contrasted with the more negotiated authority of the home.

Schools may nevertheless be seen to occupy an ambiguous position in terms of public and private social practices and orientations, at least in the earliest years of education. Overall, the educational system serves to structure the transition for children from the world of home to the world of work. In the first school, children's individual idiosyncracies, behaviours, and emotional expressions, may be tolerated to some extent, and the boundary between home and school may be blurred in a variety of ways. This can be seen, for example, in the way that parents may be allowed to come into the classroom to settle their children before leaving them, or that children may be allowed to bring some favourite toy into school as a symbolic comforter, indicating a continuity between home and school experiences. Quite quickly, however, as the years progress, the differences between home and school are made more and more apparent to children as they learn the differences between public and private social practices and orientations.

Sue Kirkpatrick interviewed mothers of 9/10 year olds about home school relations as part of her postgraduate research at

Oxford Brookes University (Kirkpatrick, 2000). Her interviews show that mothers used a very marked language of 'open-ness' when discussing relationships with their children's first schools. Even so, this open-ness may be conditional:

> ...although they've got this open policy that parents can come in... I think they're more reluctant when a disruptive parent comes in, or somebody who has different ideas about how things should be. (Diane, quoted by Kirkpatrick, 2000: 69)[3]

As these mothers experienced their children's move into middle schools[4], however, even this conditional open-ness was found to shift very significantly, with several mothers characterising this in terms of increasing 'formality', and a sense of distance. Laura particularly talked about this in terms of the power of the school. As she said in the context of her experience of wanting to talk to her child's teacher:

> I had to go to reception first, wait there... and it's very formal. Very very formal... You can't just go direct to the teacher. (*ibid*: 44)

Laura's remark also indicates how aware she felt of the power of the school to impose its own procedures and rules, and she expressed a feeling that she was losing control over her child's experiences:

> It's sort of like... 'No, we're in charge of schooling now. You're nothing to do with it'. (*ibid*: 45)

> At the first school they're very open, a very open policy, you could go in and talk to the teacher...But here, the parents aren't allowed in... (*ibid*: 42)

Besides an increasing sense of distance, formality and loss of control within the school setting itself, as the children move on there is also less scope for mothers to interact with each other and thus less social space for private practices and orientations to be shared within mothers' own networks and interactions (Bell and Ribbens, 1994).

> I just found it very weird when he started there [at middle school] that suddenly, geographically, you didn't have anything to do with the school at all. Em, and particularly that you didn't have anything to do with other parents... (Fiona, *ibid*: 47)

Many of the mothers did anticipate that there would be changes of this sort as their children moved into secondary schools, and they accepted them by reference to ideas about their children's perceived need for independence[5]. This understanding, of a need to develop into independent individuals, resonates with the more public orientation to autonomous individuality, as compared with the more private orientation to connectedness. However, the mothers had strong views about the ages at which it was appropriate for such public orientation to independent, autonomous individuality to take priority:

> Somehow the [middle] school almost treats them as though they're 11 when they start... they treat them as though it's a transition from primary to secondary, and they assume they can look after themselves a bit more than they can I think... They don't really have the sort of level of pastoral care that you might expect for nine year olds. (Fiona, *ibid*: 49)

In these respects, then, it is apparent that schools are quickly experienced by mothers as public settings in children's lives. Homes, on the other hand, are often idealised as private, a haven from the pressures of the world outside. The concepts of home and family are closely related, although by no means synonymous, and people's everyday understandings of the meaning of 'family' may themselves vary considerably. Research around the family lives of teenagers, for example (Gillies *et al*, 2001) found that the term 'family' was suffused with strong ideological overtones, and was experienced in a powerful and emotive way. We also know from research with step-families and with gay and lesbian couples, that this idealised imagery of family is one to which people may aspire and lay claim regardless of their household structure (Weeks *et al*, 1999; Ribbens McCarthy *et al*, 2003).

While it is clear that family and home constitute powerful social constructions, in their everyday accounts people often draw upon a naturalised language to describe their family lives. Families are thus conveyed as being rooted in biological imperatives and processes, but this serves to obscure the extent of the effort mothers generally expend in the construction of this supposedly natural and spontaneously occurring unit. While schools may be engaged in a variety of balancing acts around and between individual children and organisational imperatives, mothers may be engaged in balancing acts of their own. My research (Ribbens, 1994) amongst a group of women living in broadly similar socio-economic circumstances found that the women varied in their understandings and approaches to these balancing acts, but they could be understood by reference to a number of key issues:

• a balancing act between the different aspects of a child's individuality (emotional, intellectual, spiritual, social etc.)

• a balancing act around the needs of different individuals within the family unit

• a balancing act between an orientation to family members as individuals, as against an orientation to the family as a unit in itself (understood, for example, in terms of family togetherness).

These various balancing acts mean that mothers may have quite different agendas and issues to consider alongside any focus on the individual child's educational development within the home setting. Besides a concern with family issues and priorities, women may also have more varied concerns with children's non-educational needs. Kirkpatrick found great variability between mothers in terms of the extent to which they endorsed educational priorities in their children's lives, or sought to limit these:

> Some had greater concerns about emotional and welfare issues, some placed enormous priority on academic attainment, and others found the emphasis which some schools placed on SATS and 11+ unwelcome and overbearing. Some wanted their children to work at their own pace, some organised private tutors to supplement what went on at school. There was a wide variation in mothers' expectations of the things their children's school should prioritise. (2000: 84)

The child at home is thus interacting in quite a different context from the child at school, not least because childhood is understood to mean different things in different settings. And along with these variable meanings of childhood are concomitant variable implications for what it is to be an adult responsible for child/ren.[6]

Berry Mayall and Marie-Claude Foster (1989), for example, researched women as mothers and women as health visitors, and
their discussion highlights the variable concerns and understandings of these two sets of 'responsible adults'. Furthermore,
we may note, each set is placed differently in relation to public and
private ways of being, since health visitors (like teachers) are professionals working to contractual obligations for formal organisations. Mayall and Foster found that, although there were major
areas of overlap in the mothers' and health visitors' orientations to
children, there were also some very important divergences. This
could be seen particularly in terms of the knowledge base they saw
as relevant, and their time orientation. Mothers from diverse
social circumstances were thus much more concerned than health
visitors about their children's happiness in the present, and were
confident in their own knowledge of their children based in the
history of their detailed, everyday lives together, rooted in a
specific particularistic relationship. What is especially interesting is
that individuals who were *both* mothers and health visitors would
themselves prioritise their privately based knowledge in relation to
their own children, even though they would expect to prioritise
their more publicly based knowledge of children and child
development in their work as health visitors. The divergence
between publicly and privately based orientations to children may
thus be personified/internalised within the individual mother/
professional.

My argument thus far, then, is that differences between the
physical settings of home/family and school may also be understood in terms of differences between public and private social
practices and orientations. In order to understand what is going
on between mothers and schools we have to recognise this boundary and the various associated and extensive differences in terms
of the values, concerns, and ways of knowing, that are relevant on
each side. However, the concerns and knowledge bases to be
found on the public side of the boundary are manifested in powerful social practices, including the dominance of the 'psy' public
discourses and ideas about child development that underpin the
work of schools (Rose, 1990, Burman, 1994). Ironically, too, as
Gill Crozier (1998) has argued, increasing rhetoric of 'partner-

ship' and parental involvement leads inevitably to further impetus for schools to exercise surveillance over parents, and school them in the ways of 'good parenting' according to these public ways of being.

There is thus a powerful imperative for mothers to be seen to be valuing their children's educational progress, and very limited scope or space for resistance to public educational orientations. Amy, for example, saw parental involvement in their child's education as an integral part of a mother's job, using a language that comes close to that of parenthood as a lifestyle choice:

> Well, it's the responsibility of parents – okay, you don't always make a decision to have a baby, but in this day and age, if you make a decision to produce that baby, it's up to you do to your best for it, and doing your best includes involving yourself in its education. (Kirkpatrick, 2000: 78)

This comment is paralleled in the study by Yvette Solomon *et al* (2002) which focused on homework issues with children in their early teens. They found that 53% of the parents they interviewed saw helping with homework as an integral part of the parental role. Mothers/parents may thus see educational issues, such as homework, as an inevitable and quite taken-for-granted part of the parenting 'caringscape' (McKie *et al*, 2002).

Much of this public dominance in discourses and practices around parenting occurs in subtle ways, with shifts in language that constantly extend the reach of public orientations, and re-frame private understandings in these terms. This can be seen, for example, in the recent pervasive and powerful introduction of the language of parenting 'skills'. This language builds upon the longer established re-framing of mothers' relationships with their children in terms of the public language of 'work'.7 The notion of parenting skills conveys the idea that mothering involves a set of techniques which can be imparted in education and training programmes, rendering invisible other understandings of mothering as an on-going (particularistic) relationship.

We thus see, on the one hand, powerful public understandings of what it means to be a mother of a child as school pupil and future worker and citizen, and on the other hand, powerful imagery of what it means to be a mother of a child in a family setting. But while imagery of family and home is undoubtedly very significant in contemporary Western societies, material, cultural and household diversity means that there is considerable variability as to how far, and whether, mothers themselves seek to draw a clear boundary around their families and homes, and how far they themselves may experience authority as well as responsibility within this private space. In the UK context, we have seen quite a shift in recent years in legislative and policy terms, from an emphasis upon parental authority to one of parental responsibility (Ribbens, 1992). In educational arenas, the emphasis on parental responsibility can be seen too in relation to ideas of home-school agreements, or minimum hours of homework. But policy still carries a fine balance around the expectation that while parents may owe it to their children to exercise their responsibilities for them, once they do fulfil their obligations, parents themselves are entitled to freedom from outside interference in carrying out those obligations. The notion of responsibility thus carries the potential to confer authority, an authority that may be compromised by any help or interference from outside.

There is therefore scope for considerable variability between mothers in terms of how far they may expect continuity or sharp differentiation in a child's experience between the home and the school. Even in my research (Ribbens, 1994) with mothers living in broadly similar socio-economic circumstances, I found considerable variability between women in terms of how they viewed their family boundaries, and their own role in mediating these boundaries. This could be understood particularly around two key issues:

1. Do women expect continuity or discontinuity between children's experiences at home and at school? Do they thus perceive a weak or strong boundary between home and school, private and public? And where they do expect continuity between the two settings, do they expect this continuity to flow from home experiences into school lives, or from school lives into home life?

2. How far do women feel able to be assertive in the public setting of the school? Do they assert their own ideas and authority about their children's educational experiences, or do they defer to professional ideas about children's educational needs?

These two key issues can be seen to cross cut, to create a four-fold typology of potential home-school relationships from the mothers' perspectives:

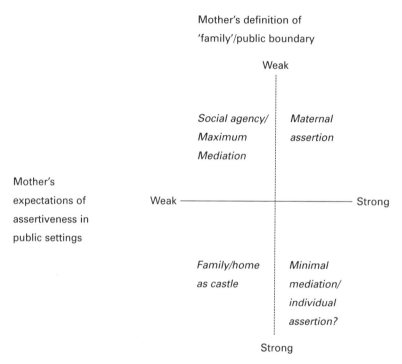

Maternal assertion occurs where the boundary definition is weak, so that mothers expect continuity between home and school, and where mothers are assertive towards school settings. Continuity between home and school thus depends on the assumption that expectations developed within the home may be extended to the school. However, such assertion may require high levels of resources and confidence in the ability to speak out, which may be characterised in confrontational terms of being 'forthright' or going in 'all guns blazing' (Diane and Sue, quoted by Kirkpatrick, 2000: 23-4). Even so, mothers may express a feeling that their power to change things in schools is in fact quite limited in the face of the formality and bureaucracy of the public educational system.

Social agency/maximum participation also occurs where the boundary definition is weak, but where the mother's attitude towards the school is less assertive and more deferential. Expectations based upon children's school lives are thus taken into the home, and used as a basis for social practices and orientations towards family lives.

In many respects, this is the form of maternal mediation that we might expect schools to see as most desirable. Homework is one obvious example in which such maternal/parental social agency may be expected, and practised, on a broad scale, as a general feature of parenting, discussed further below.

The family/home as castle occurs where there is a strong boundary definition, so that the family/home is defined as a different sort of setting from school. However, the mother here does not take an assertive attitude outside the home, so that children are expected to defer to publicly based practices and orientations when at school. This weak level of assertion outside the home is limited, however, by the private boundary. At home, then, more privately based practices and orientations, based upon family lives and experiences, may be given priority.

Individual assertion/minimal mediation again involves a strong boundary definition but in combination with an assertive attitude outside the home. While different expectations may be seen as relevant to school life and home life, then, this need not mean that the individual is expected to defer to others. There is likely to be a more open question here about what expectations should in fact operate in the child's school life, but it seems likely that the mother here adopts a minimal mediatory role, leaving the child to assert her own expectations in school.

Home-school boundaries in everyday lives – resistance from the private?

In this final section, I consider empirical work that may be used to exemplify some of these more abstract theoretical ideas that I have discussed so far. I start by exploring case studies of women from my earlier work (Ribbens, 1993, 1994), and then consider further the recent empirical work undertaken by Sue Kirkpatrick (2000).

The case study women are drawn from a larger group of women interviewed, who all had an eldest child aged 7, and all lived in the South East of England outside London. The third woman described here was interviewed specifically because she had made particular educational choices for her children, as will become apparent.

Maternal assertion – Kate was happy to hear professional advice in relation to her children, as long as it did not threaten her maternal authority. When her eldest child started school, there were some difficulties which had not been experienced while he was at nursery school, because the primary school seemed to be operating with a different model of learning from the one Kate preferred, of waiting for the child to be ready to learn. She therefore changed his school, to obtain the continuity she sought between her own views and those of the school, and had indeed sought out different schools for each of her three children to suit their individual needs. She thus had the confidence actively to seek out and assert her own educational preferences for her children. Nevertheless, her own authority was constrained by various limits, e.g. of not actually knowing what was going on at school during the day, and of having to shape family routines and priorities around school timetables and priorities.

Social agency – Shirley recounted happy stories of her life with her two children when they were very small, and expressed a concern to meet her children's needs with as little restriction as possible. But, while Shirley at times expressed quite strong views of home and school as different settings, she trod a gentle line in her relationship with the school and generally expected to fulfil the educational activities she believed were wanted of her as a mother at home. Both health and education were matters in which she respected the advice of professionals. She gave education some centrality in her account of her childrearing, and was pleased to undertake educational activities at home. Nevertheless, she also set clear limits to the goal of using education to progress in life: 'If it's going to upset the children, then I don't think it's worth it'. Shirley was concerned that the teachers should think well of her as a mother. She went into school weekly to help with cooking, and tried not to make undue demands. She saw going to see the headmaster as 'making waves', and most of her contact with teachers occurred at the initiative of the teachers themselves, who expressed concerns about the children not being able to speak up for themselves.

The family/home as castle – This view of the family school boundary was apparent in the accounts of a number of women in my research, who might see family and school as quite different settings, be quite deferential to educational authority within school, but might use a strong family boundary to defend a social space for their children to experience a different way of being. This occurred in its starkest form with Emily, who had not found any organised setting outside her home where she felt confident about handing over her children to someone else's authority and care. Consequently Emily's children had never attended any formal schooling, and had never crossed the boundary into a public institutional structure. Emily felt a marked contrast between the ways in which they lived their family life, and the demands that school would make:

> He couldn't have coped with the discipline of school because we've led such an undisciplined life really, with few constraints or things put upon him, that he has to do things. He could do what he chose to do.

By not sending the children to school, Emily had avoided their encounter with school structures and values, and had also kept her home life free from the constraints other mothers learn to take for granted. Emily had decided not to compromise her family life by entering into such relationships with an outside authority.

Minimal mediation – Janet similarly regarded home and school as separate spheres, and had an uneasy relationship with her child's teachers. Janet made it clear that she found great enjoyment in the company of her son, Russell, and had few problems in her relationship with him, particularly at home or in the local neighbourhood. In relation to Russell's school life, Janet did expect teachers to exert discipline in schools, but she regarded home as a different sort of setting from school:

> I suppose discipline's alright at school, because otherwise you're going to have them bashing the teachers or something... but you don't want that at home as well, you've got to have a bit of leeway.

Nevertheless, Janet did express her concerns about Russell's education, and her willingness to work with him at home, although she did not have confidence about this. Yet her contacts with teachers had not always been easy, and she expressed resentment at some of the negative comments she had received from teachers

> ...my impression was that Mrs M and Mrs S didn't like him, so they obviously thought, well, why should we help him?

Here, then, we see that although there was shared agreement about the importance of learning, there could be different conceptions of the nature of the child concerned, and of the role of the teacher. The role of the teacher is seen as very different from the role of the mother, and home is seen as quite different from school, but Janet was unwilling to defer to the teachers and resisted their perspectives on her son. The boundary here between home and school is quite sharply defined, with considerable potential for tension, despite good will on both sides.

Having considered these different approaches to maternal mediation of the home school boundary, what general points can we draw about the issues that may cut across the boundaries between home and school? In what ways do schools affect home lives, and how may parents in return seek to affect schools, or at least to resist school practices and orientations?

It seems clear that what goes on in schools can have significant implications for children's family lives. For example, how far do mothers themselves, in their family lives at home, consider what sorts of social and educational skills children are going to need to survive and thrive within the educational system? And what sorts of implications do children's school based identities have for interactions within families? Annette Lareau (1989), for example, points out the significant implications for sibling relationships when one child is seen as doing better at school than another. There are also major issues about how school time shapes family time. As home-school agreements make explicit, attendance at school requires the child's punctual appearance at a particular site at a pre-ordained and regular time dictated by the requirements of organisational co-ordination. Family time within its own terms may, at least for some families, provide some scope for ideas about 'going with the flow', and experiencing freedom from clock watching and timetables, responding to the on-going needs of people in the family as these are expressed, as in the case of Emily above. This is a view of time that is likely to be more available for most mothers during school holidays.

A major issue that has increasingly become a priority within public policy is homework, the implications of which for family life seem to go largely unremarked.[8] Parents are expected to support these school-defined endeavours without comment, and, on the whole, they seem to do so. Studies that seek parents' accounts of how they manage homework as a feature of family life are sparse, but even here, may often still leave the value of homework as a desirable practice virtually unchallenged (e.g. Levin *et al*, 1997). These studies do, however, clearly point to considerable variation in the views and experiences of parents as regards homework, though its widespread salience as a topic is apparent in its spontaneous discussion in research interviews about parenting (Solomon *et al*, 2002). While some parents find pleasure in supporting their child's homework, many doubt their own adequacy as educators, describe the time management difficulties it creates, and generally discuss it as a source of sometimes extreme tension and conflict (Levin *et al*, 1997; Hallam and Cowan, 2000; Kralovec and Buell, 2000, 2001; Solomon *et al*, 2002).[9] In the UK context, as Solomon *et al* (2002) discuss, policy tends to consider homework as critically important, but fails to recognise the possibility that it may create tensions and anxiety in family relationships. Indeed, as these authors conclude:

> Current government initiatives relating to homework reflect the wider background concern with parenting which, despite the rhetoric of support for families, is based on a deficit model frequently positioning parents as irresponsible and ill-informed. (2002:620)

In the context of my present discussion, however, what is significant is not so much the rights and wrongs of homework as a desirable practice, but rather the ways in which mothers may have to mediate these issues in their everyday lives, and whether or not they find any scope for resisting public discourse, or prioritising more privately based ways of being with children.

In Kirkpatrick's research (2000), when mothers were asked what they felt was expected of them as parents by the school, homework was one of the first things that many women mentioned and its significance was clear in their daily interactions with their children within the home and family. The rhetoric of good parenting, and the desire by mothers to be seen accordingly by schools, may make it hard for parents to voice, or even think, any resistance to these practices. No parent wants to be seen as anything less than supportive of their children, whatever their circumstances[10].

Yet, in research interviews or in private conversations, parents may at some point express their resentment at having family boundaries invaded in this way, to the point of outright anger at a feeling that parents are being asked to do the school's job for them.

> ...sometimes, if he's forgotten something and he's in tears at nine o'clock at night and he hasn't done it, I just think, well, what the hell are we doing here?... I find homework a complete pain actually. We both work full time... and I've got a three year old as well, so when I get home from work I want to have some time... and you know, he's at school all day – give him a break! I don't agree with them getting homework in the holidays either, 'cos I think, well... he'll get there... there's enough time between now and when he's 16 to get there. (Lorraine, *ibid*: 79)

Similarly, in a private conversation to which I was myself witness, I have heard several middle class mothers complain particularly vociferously when their primary schools set homework for children during the half term holiday. One of these women was herself a parent governor, but still felt unable to voice her feelings as she assumed that this position meant she should be seen to be supporting the school's decisions. But the mothers saw this as breaching a boundary that should have been respected, for freedom from educational responsibilities for themselves and their children, and to provide a space for family togetherness around leisure time. Mothers may also feel that homework during term time should take its place alongside other activities within their children's lives.

Some of the mothers in Sue Kirkpatrick's interviews discussed ways in which they sought to manage or limit the impact of homework on their children's home lives, reflecting a view that '...homework is a good thing, but I think there is... too much' (Diane, as quoted by Kirkpatrick, 2000: 75). Nevertheless, mothers also discussed how they felt there was very little scope for resistance so that schools pushed them into behaving as quasi-teachers, a role in which they might feel uncomfortable. Yet schools' powerful position in the lives of their children might make women feel they had little real choice. Laura discussed her resistance to the expectation that she should sign her daughter's homework book:

> I'm not going to write, 'Yes, she's done her homework'... I can't really see... the teacher knows she's done her homework, she either knows that she has or she hasn't... but Emily did come home the other day and said, 'Oh, my teacher says if you don't sign my homework book I'll get a pink slip, and well, if you get two pink slips you get a detention. And I said to her, well, nobody's going to give you a detention because I haven't signed a piece of paper... I mean it's very strange. (*ibid*: 76)

Laura's quote highlights another dilemma for mothers in mediating these home school boundaries: that there may be others whose actions and views are relevant, and which the women may actively mediate, whether they come from children or (ex) partners.

How then do parents seek to exert any control or have any effect on what is going on in schools? Approaching teachers and schools even for advice or information may be seen by parents as a delicate line to tread. Parents may feel vulnerable to teachers' comments and judgements, and as lacking in basic knowledge of what is, or should be, occurring during their children's school experiences. Parents may have considerable anxieties about antagonising teachers, or being out of their depth on educational issues.

Where parents are unhappy with the outcome of contact with schools, they may seek out other resources to supplement school education or to reinforce their own points of view, such as other professional assessments. Another common approach is to try to become more involved with the school, developing closer relationships with teachers and gaining greater knowledge about school activities. This may involve mothers in converting the formal public relationship between mother and teacher into a less formal private relationship – as a friendship. Sally discussed how involvement on the PTA could be useful in this way:

> ...the barriers go down a bit, and you do get to know them more as people rather than as somebody's teacher. Like they get to know us, I suppose, rather than as somebody's mum. (*ibid*: 62)

However, the ambiguities in this sort of relationship, and the inescapable awareness of different interests that are associated on either side of the home school boundary, can restrict this approach. When Sally talked about her friendship with her daughter's teacher she was quite clear about this:

> There are definite set parameters... I wouldn't compromise our friendship by asking ... difficult questions. (*ibid*: 58)

Conclusions

Parents may feel in a cleft stick at times, torn between wanting to protect their children from the harshness and one-sidedness of school demands on their children's emotional and physical lives, while also wanting their children to do well, and so at times adding to the pressure. The study of middle class families by Jordan *et al*, suggested that the...

> ...paradox of their lives was not the constraint associated with riches, but the self-defeating pursuit of advantage. Putting the family first implied that they had to take every step available to give their children a better chance of making something of themselves than other people's children enjoyed... the logic of their choices must always tend to towards giving their offspring a head-

start... over others who would also be striving to make something of themselves. (1994: 222)

Indeed, one of the arguments made against homework is that it deepens class divisions (eg Levin *et al*, 1997; Kralovec and Buell, 2001).

While the content of the issues around the lives of mothers and schools may thus vary considerably according to women's material, cultural and household circumstances, there are always likely to be tensions around the home school boundary regardless of circumstances. This is not to gloss over the significant differences that arise between women from different social contexts in their relations with schools (see e.g. Crozier, 1997, 2000; Reay, 1998), but to try and maintain a space for seeing other issues too, based in other frames of reference that are almost certainly more significantly shaped by gender.[11]

As various writers have discussed (eg Balloch and Taylor, 2001; Clarke and Glendinning, 2002), the political rhetoric of partnership around public services has remained strong under various governments in recent British history, even while the content of the rhetoric may shift. As Susan Balloch and Marilyn Taylor point out, however, it requires a critical perspective to analyse the assumptions behind such rhetoric:

> Partnership reflects ideals of participatory democracy and equality between partners. It assumes overarching common interests between different players and it can underplay the difficulties in bringing together different interests and different cultures. (2001: 2)

Furthermore, the power differentials underlying the practices of 'partnership' can be argued to constitute a new form of (indirect) state control through 'governance' (Clarke and Glendinning, 2002). Here, I have explored the expectations, taken-for-granted assumptions, and tensions that may be involved in mothers' mediations of home-school boundaries, rooted in different public and private ways of being, and the possible scope for resistance to such governance. A real partnership between home and school would not seek to gloss over the tensions, but perhaps accept them as inevitable, and use any 'partnership' to consider where and how all the parties involved feel it is desirable to draw the boundary.

In the context of the compulsory education system, the policy language of partnership (and, it must be added, most of the research literature on parent-school relations), is entirely framed by reference to a focus on children's educational achievements in schools, providing no space for the recognition of alternative, privately based ways of being. To be able to understand the context for mothers' concerns about their children's school lives, we need to maintain a theoretical space so we can see that there may be other things going on, underpinned by private social practices and orientations. The private is a particular 'way of being' that is distinct from public understandings, and mothers are involved in complex balancing acts in mediating these different settings and their associated practices and understandings. Schools as institutions are clearly located within public ways of being, even though this position may be compromised to some degree at the very beginnings of the educational structures that shape a child's school life.

Women as mothers mediate these different aspects of the boundaries between public and private in different ways, in the context of individual experiences and value systems, and diverse material, cultural and household circumstances. Whatever their circumstances, however, there are always likely to be tensions associated with such boundaries and there is seldom scope for resistance to the power of the school's more public way of being.

Notes

1 The first person is used to refer to Jane Ribbens McCarthy.

2 For an alternative, more 'layered', way of discussing public and private, see Ribbens McCarthy and Edwards, 2000, 20002).

3 This perception is perhaps particularly significant when set against professional advice that the effectiveness of a home-school policy can be judged by the extent to which 'parents start to ask awkward questions' (Workshop on Partnership with Parents, 1997).

4 In two of the educational authorities where Kirkpatrick has located her sample, there is a system of transferring to middle schools before moving on to secondary schools. This may be relevant to why the mothers expressed strong feelings about the ways in which such educational structures may or may not reflect what they consider to be appropriate age related expectations.

5 Research with the parents of young people shows that independence is a theme that is seen as central to the teenage years, though its meaning may vary (Gillies *et al*, 2001).

6 We should also explicitly acknowledge that this paper is itself not focused on children *per se*, but on the roles of some of those adults who are socially constructed as res-

ponsible for children. For a different perspective on the education system, arising from a focus on children themselves, see, for example, Mayall (2003) *Sociologies of Childhood and Educational Thinking*, Professorial lecture, October, Institute of Education.

7 See Ribbens McCarthy and Edwards (2002) for a discussion of the gains and losses in the use of this language by feminist writers about women's lives as mothers.

8 As this chapter went to press, however, this issue did gain attention in the regional BBC news (11.02.04, London Breakfast News), in response to a publication by Hallam (2004).

9 In the study of Solomon *et al* (2002) views varied from the 14% of parents who enjoyed involvement in their children's homework, through those 20% who regarded themselves as 'wholly inadequate in homework support' (p610), to those 20% who positioned themselves as acting on behalf of the child, 'sometimes against the explicit 'common enemy' of school' (p612).

10 Children's views on these matters are even less vocalised (although see the work of Edwards and Alldred (2000) and Edwards (2002) on the views of children generally about the home school boundary.

11 There has not been space here to consider how social differences such as class and ethnicity may themselves significantly relate in variable ways to women's understandings and experiences of public and private. See Ribbens McCarthy and Edwards, (2002) for a more extended discussion of some of these issues.

5

Participation, Inequality, Self-interest

Anne Phillips

The essays in this book address a variety of forms of parental involvement, and a number signal concerns about the effects in practice of what in principle seem eminently desirable goals. My focus here is on forms of participation that enable parents to influence school policy and practice: involvement, most notably, in governing bodies. I start with two examples, constructed as a composite from the experience of a number of schools, and based partly on anecdotal evidence. The status of the examples is illustrative, though the relevance of the issues raised is borne out by the wider literature (e.g. Deem *et al*, 1995; Blackledge, 1995; Crozier, 2000). I draw on these to explore a number of themes relating to participation, representation, and deliberation.

School A is an inner city school that exhibits many of the characteristics of schools in poorer neighbourhoods. Its buildings are in urgent need of improvement and repair; it has difficulty recruiting and keeping qualified staff; many of its pupils come from families where English is not the first language; and performance in Key Stage Three tests is well below the national average. In accordance with what were till recently the national guidelines[1], the governing body was supposed to include four or five parents elected by parents of pupils currently at the school, three or four people appointed by the LEA, one or two teachers elected by and from the teachers, one member of the non-teaching staff, three or four co-optees designed to reflect a balance of community and other interests, and where s/he wishes, the school head. The composition is intended, in other words, to ensure that those working at the school have roughly equal representation with parents whose children study there, with the weight, if anything, going to the latter; and in normal circumstances, teaching and non-teaching staff would make up at most 25% of the governing body. In School A, however, there have been chronic difficulties finding people willing to act as governors. There are vacancies in nearly every category – for parent governors, co-opted governors, as well as those appointed by the LEA – and even when new governors are recruited, they often find it hard to attend the meetings. This last has proved particularly difficult for parent governors. The result is that those working at the school are the only fully represented group on the governing body. Indeed, since the co-optees and parent governors also include past employees of the school, it sometimes seems that representation is entirely in the hands of insiders. This over-representation of one category need not matter – and on many issues will not – but is clearly not what was intended.

School B enjoys considerably more favourable circumstances: a buildings programme that is steadily enhancing its facilities; a middle class catchment area that provides it with (reasonably) well motivated and well supported children; and results at GCSE and A level that are significantly above the national average. The composition of the governing body is again designed to ensure only minority representation for those working at the school. There were supposed to be six parent governors, five LEA appointees, two teachers, one representative of non-teaching staff, up to five co-optees, and where s/he wishes, the headteacher. For school B, there is never a problem finding people willing to serve as parent governor; all vacancies are contested, and those elected are regular in their attendance. Many governors are in professional employment, and the school can draw on an impressive array of financial, educational and fund-raising skills. Representation is heavily skewed towards these middle class parents, whose preoccupations include tightening up homework schedules, addressing problems of drug abuse, and further improving exam results. In School B, there is plenty of pressure from the governing body pushing the school to identify remaining areas of weakness and develop strategies for improvement; and though the pressure comes mainly from middle class governors, most parents will want their children to work hard and steer clear of drugs, and there is no reason to see these preoccupations as unrepresentative. Except, that is, for one notable gap. The school has never been particularly good at inspiring its more disaffected and/or less academic pupils, tending rather to rely on the steady stream of well-motivated students, and wait for the others to drop out or leave. It seems plausible to suspect a class bias here, for while disaffection is by no means restricted to working class pupils, its long term effects on life-chances are particularly dramatic for those from the working class.

As the examples suggest, models drawn up for enhanced parental or community participation can founder on structural constraints that lead to the over-representation of certain groups and under-representation of others. When we regard this as a problem, it is primarily because we think that different groups have different concerns – if this were not the case, school government could be safely left in the hands of teachers and educational experts, employing what we hope to be their superior knowledge to promote what we assume to be common concerns. Distrust of this last scenario reflects a widely shared perception that teachers and/or educational experts have their own agenda. It reflects a perception, that is, that there are different groups and that each of these can have different priorities and concerns. Enhanced participation is sometimes invoked precisely so as to empower this wider diversity of interests; but as the experience of schools A and B indicate, enhanced participation does not always work out as planned. One might, indeed, suggest that both schools would be better served if control over educational policy and practice reverted to the much maligned LEA: that staff at school A would then be more rigorously regulated; and staff at school B required to demonstrate that they are addressing *all* their pupils' needs.

This is not the flavour of the day in British educational thinking, where recent consultation on the composition of school governing bodies has led to new guidelines (set out in the 2002 Education Act) that will reduce the number of LEA governors and increase the proportion of parent governors. Nor, indeed, is it the argument I wish pursue here. There are important and compelling arguments for increased parental participation, including:

1) that parents will provide more sustained support for the work of teachers if they feel they have had some voice in formulating school policy and practice (the argument from efficiency)

2) that teachers will be better able to identify and address the needs of individual children if they listen to what parents can tell them (the argument from communication)

3) that parents will be better placed than distant policy-makers or administrators to identify the strengths and weaknesses of their child's school, and particularly well placed to suggest improvements (the argument from local knowledge)

4) that enhanced participation by parents can make educational practice more responsive to local circumstances or needs and better tuned in to ethnic and cultural diversity (the argument from diversity)

5) that enhanced participation by parents can even out the chances for less powerful groups to influence decisions (the argument from equality).

I endorse, to varying degrees, all of these arguments. Yet it is clear from the examples set out above that participation has its hazards, and cannot be invoked without qualification as the only road to pursue. I address here two major areas of concern: first, the difficulties in achieving fair representation; and secondly, whether participation can lend itself to the promotion of narrowly personal or group gain.

Participation and inequality

The first problem (contrary to the hope expressed in the fifth argument for participation) is that those who participate are always a skewed sub-set of those entitled to participate: skewed sometimes by gender, sometimes by race, and virtually always by social class. This remains true even in relation to voting in national elections, one of the more minimal forms of participation, consuming barely ten minutes in every four to five years; and the discrepancies between groups typically increase as the participation becomes more demanding. There is a large literature on political participation confirming this point (e.g Parry *et al*, 1992; Beetham *et al*, 2002), but it is hardly necessary to refer to it, for the reasons are relatively easy to find. The skewing of participation is partly a matter of time, as when parents juggling the care of their children with long hours in employment find themselves cutting out all extraneous activities. More insidiously, it also reflects people's assumptions about their own competencies: whether they think they know anything about the issues under discussion, whether they think they have something worthwhile to say.

Though some of the variation comes down to quirks of personality, there is a strong correlation between levels of educational achievement and the kind of self-confidence that propels people into civic or political activity. Since levels of educational achievement remains closely tied to class origin (Marshall, Swift and Roberts, 1997), it is hardly surprising that participation levels should be skewed in favour of the middle class, or that rates of volunteering should be twice as high for professional and managerial groups as for manual workers (Gaskin and Davis Smith, 1997). In periods of robust trade union or party mobilisation, this tendency was balanced by counter-movements that encouraged high levels of activity and involvement among those who felt themselves most excluded from the corridors of power. One of the worries about our own era is that these counter-tendencies have become less effective. In this context, levels of educational achievement threaten to become the primary determinant of who participates in political and social life.

In the relationship between gender and participation, there is also a historic shift that promises to alter the conditions for participation. In an earlier period, women were less likely than men to gain educational qualifications and less likely to perceive themselves as having competences outside the domestic/familial sphere; for those with significant child care responsibilities, there were also severe constraints of time. But this was in part countered by the lower proportion of women working in full time jobs outside the home, which generated significant numbers of women offering their services in the voluntary sector, in parent-teacher associations and other forms of community involvement. There have been major and much discussed changes on all these fronts: most notably, a marked increase in women's labour force parti-cipation; an equalisation between the sexes in educational achieve-ments; an equalisation (not yet complete) in self-perceptions of competence; and a reduction in average family size. The overall result is that the gender gap in social and political participation has significantly closed (though less so at the higher levels of political influence and power), but that women are less available now for contributions at local and community level.

Analysts of 'social capital' have argued that full-time work in-creases women's participation in work or professional associa-tions, but inhibits their more social involvement. Indeed, com-menting on the decline in community engagement in the USA, Robert Putnam (2000:201) suggests that 'one practical way to increase community engagement in America would be to make it easier for women (and men too) to work part-time if they wished'. The afterthought of the bracketed men suggests a nostalgia for a world where women were primarily located in the home, but we need not delay to debate this nostalgia, for it is unlikely that the modern economy will facilitate such a reversal of trends. With many households now dependent on two full incomes, we can more realistically anticipate an equalisation between the sexes in the propensity to get involved in parent-teacher associations or school governing bodies, but an overall deficit of participants. We can perhaps also anticipate that the tendency of either sex to parti-cipate will increasingly correlate with higher social class and educational qualifications.

These features reflect structural characteristics of the wider economy and society, and the impact these have on whether individuals become involved; and they provide us with the first set of problems regarding the incidence of participation. The second set arises more internally from the process of participation itself. Part of the skewing of involvement across different groups is that those who *have* become involved will often generate their own forms of exclusivity. This can make it difficult for those hovering on the edges to feel at home within the group.

This problem was much rehearsed in the early years of the contemporary women's movement (e.g. Freeman, 1985; Mansbridge, 1980; Phillips, 1991), when seemingly egalitarian practices of participatory democracy came to be perceived as deeply exclusionary by working class and black feminists. Most of the women's groups that formed through the late 1960s and 1970s were committed to informal, supposedly non-hierarchical structures; indeed, in a frequently invoked comparison, women's group meetings were patterned on a gathering of friends. But while the blurring of boundaries between politics and friendship contributed much to the energy and excitement of the movement, it also tended to create an exclusionary magic circle, an informal caucus that helped sustain hidden structures of power. For those already involved in a group, the informality, shared references, and shared lifestyle were a major attraction, but for those not yet included in the circle, they constituted a powerful barrier. This was particularly problematic when the original members were also so similar in age, class and race: mostly in their twenties and thirties, mostly university educated, and overwhelmingly white.

For critics of participatory democracy, the tendency to recruit activists from an unrepresentative sub-group – and then generate informal barriers that make it even harder for others to join in – is one damning indictment. The result, it is sometimes suggested, is that participation promotes a new kind of elitism, in which 'the few do better and count for more, than the passive, inert, apathetic, nonparticipant many' (Sartori, 1987: 114). Part of the argument here is that those who choose to participate are likely to hold unusually strong views. That this might be so is hardly surprising, for those who participate are almost by definition people who have put more thought into the issues than the average citizen; and it would be odd to disparage them for this. We might, on the contrary, feel we would rather have the active and engaged making the decisions that shape our lives than the passive, apathetic and inert. But if the views these represent are significantly at odds with the views of the nonparticipant many, this might give cause for concern.

It is sometimes suggested that members of political parties occupy more stark positions on a left-right axis than the voters who elect that party into power; thus that Labour Party members are more left-wing than Labour Party voters, and Conservative party members more right-wing than the average Conservative voter. One of the few comprehensive studies of Labour Party members (Seyd and Whiteley, 1992) concludes that this is just 'cheap propaganda', and that there is only a minority of issues on which party members diverge significantly from party voters. But if there were such a pattern, then opening up more space for citizen involvement could mean empowering those who hold particularly unrepresentative views. Critics might say that if we want policies that represent the average not just the activist voter, we should give up on fantasies of participation as a way of strengthening accountability or increasing popular engagement, and return to a more minimalist conception of democracy that at least gives everyone an equal vote. We should vote for our preferred party at the general election, but then leave the rest for the government to decide.

Translated to the level of schools, this would mean that the basic parameters of educational policy and practice would be settled in the course of a general election (and if not the policies, then at least the people with the authority to determine them), and not be open to subsequent disruption or distortion by parental pressure in individual schools. This is, in truth, quite close to current practice, though not at all to current rhetoric, which more commonly invokes participation as a positive good. It is not a position I would endorse, for all the reasons set out earlier in the paper. The question is not whether increasing parental involvement in schools is valuable, but whether the visions that underpin this can, in practice, be achieved.

Participation as self-interest

A further point raised by Diane Reay (see chapter 2) is that 'the concerns of involved parents are often narrow and aimed primarily at gaining advantage for their own children'. This speaks to a major concern about parental involvement, for if people are becoming involved *as parents*, with this aspect of their identity explicitly to the fore, there is almost a deliberate invitation to them to assess all issues in relation to their own children's needs. In extreme form, this might mean that the parent of tennis star Janey only supports initiatives aimed at improving school sports, while the parent of maths genius Jimmy thinks it a waste of time to organise swimming trips. What then of the process of deliberation through which governors supposedly arrive at balanced educational judgements?

The issues here reflect what has become a substantial preoccupation in the literature on democracy, where theorists have found themselves torn between the need to ensure that all citizens are equally enabled to voice their own priorities and preoccupations, and a disturbed recognition that this can promote a politics of self or group interest that fails to engage with wider concerns. When John Rawls (1971) developed his influential theory of justice, he suggested that we think of ourselves as reaching decisions from behind a 'veil of ignorance', so forgetting for the moment about our own personal circumstances and focusing on what would be a reasonable resolution for anyone, whoever they happened to be. Rawls was particularly concerned with issues about the distribution of income (what, for example, would we think to be a fair system of taxation if we did not yet know whether we were going to be at the upper or lower end of the income scale?); and how to address matters of religious and cultural difference (what position would we take on the place of religion in schools if we did not yet know whether we ourselves were religious believers, or to which religion we might belong?). Obvious extensions in the educational context would include what position we would adopt on selectivity or streaming if we did not yet know whether our children were going to be among the more or the less academic; or what position we would adopt on special measures for the education of boys or girls if we did not yet know the sex of our child.

There is an immediate plausibility to Rawls' suggestion, which draws on the distaste for special pleading and distrust of people who abuse positions of power to promote personal advantage. As applied to the current situation in schools, it would mean appealing to governors to participate not as parents but as citizens, and consider all the issues from an impartial point of view. And yet as Young (1990a) has argued, premature appeals to impartiality can work to silence the more disadvantaged, and the very value of participation may be nullified if people feel themselves compelled to express an impartial point of view.

As indicated earlier, it is part of the rationale for broadening participation that this should make it possible for people who were previously disregarded to articulate and press what may be their very different priorities and concerns. This has been regarded as an important counter-weight to an elitist welfarism that sought to determine people's needs from on high. Much of the critique of the post-war welfare state has centred on its failure to recognise citizens as participants, its tendency to position them as people with needs who must then be protected by a paternalist state (for different versions of this argument, see Habermas, 1996; Marquand, 1997; Young, 1990a). In relation to education, housing, and health, it has been argued that agendas were too exclusively determined by the professionals working in these sectors, one of the classic illustrations from post-war British housing policy being the preference for demolishing sub-standard city slums and relocating people to what architects saw as superior new housing estates but that residents often loathed. There is a cynical side to the current enthusiasm for participation, for in reducing the influence of professional associations or trade union or local councils, it potentially replaces them by isolated individuals who are unable to wield so much power. But at its best, it corrects for an elitist welfarism that failed to listen to what people actually said.

How, then, to marry these two concerns: how to give people a voice *as parents*, articulating concerns and preoccupations that might have been ignored by teachers or local councillors or educational experts? how, at the same time, to prevent them making decisions as parents of their own particular child? Part of the resolution lies in a re-assessment of the ideals of impartiality.

When people engage in politics in ways that seem to promote their own interests, when they look at things primarily from their own perspective – or as in Reay's observation, get involved in schools primarily to promote their own children's needs – we tend to think of this as demonstrating narrow self-interest. We disparage the partiality; we wish that people could look beyond their own narrow experiences to consider things from a broader point of view. The problem, however, is that this injunction against partiality may also work to silence the most disadvantaged. There is a coercive element in appeals to a general interest or common good that can operate to suppress diversity and difference, making it particularly difficult for those on the margins to articulate what they may acknowledge to be their own more specific concerns.

Iris Young (1990a) argues persuasively that the dominant groups within any society are more able to present their concerns and pre-occupations as a generalised common sense, such that they seem to be representing the requirements of justice or the dictates of efficiency. Other less powerful groups seem by contrast to be calling for special treatment or harping on their own limited concerns. It is, in other words, easier for people to present themselves as impartial or 'professional' if the positions they defend fit broadly with the *status quo*; and easier to dismiss people as promoting a particular or special interest when they are challenging norms that have been so long dominant that they have come to seem the 'natural' point of view. If so, then the injunction against particularity – the calling on people to put themselves behind a veil of ignorance, or to think beyond their own localised experiences as female or ethnic minority or poor – can work to sustain inequality between social groups. It will make it appear as if they are the ones asking for special treatment, while the 'special' treatment long provided for the others is rendered invisible by its very familiarity. It will be women or members of a minority ethnic group who are seen as pursuing partial objectives, while the partiality of other groups drops from view.

And the anxieties generated by this can have a significantly dampening effect, such that people may come to feel themselves least able to speak out on matters that are of the most pressing personal concern. It is not, I think, uncommon to feel particularly silenced on issues where others know we have an urgent personal interest, for we do not want to be seen as engaged in special pleading, and sometimes find ourselves restricting our interventions to issues on which no one could imagine we had any axe to grind. This perverse form of self-censorship testifies to the coercive power of notions of impartiality. It is easy to see how this can work to suppress awkward opinions and sustain a false consensus.

With such issues in mind, a number of theorists have argued that we need to give more explicit recognition to difference. If we are seeking to ensure that *all* social groups get an equal voice in influencing policy and practice, we can hardly do this without first acknowledging the existence of different social groups. In the context of schools, this is usually taken to mean parents, teachers, educational experts and representatives of 'the' local community; but with my comments on inequalities in participation in mind, it needs further sub-division to include social differences of gender, ethnicity, religion and class. If the aim of the exercise is to give voice to these different experiences, we can hardly hope to achieve this if we refuse to take seriously arguments that are framed with reference to these experiences.

To take a parallel argument from the world of political representation, we are unlikely to achieve equity of representation between women and men if we continue with the fiction that sex is an irrelevant consideration in the choice of party candidates. And if we see greater equity of representation as leading to policies that more fairly address women's needs or experiences, we cannot realistically combine this with disparaging those women representatives who harp on about women's 'narrow' needs or concerns. Acknowledging group difference is often the first step towards addressing group inequality. Refusing to acknowledge it often reinforces the *status quo* (Phillips, 1995).

What, however, of the dangers from the other side? As opponents of gender or ethnic quotas frequently argue, the use of group categories to promote a more inclusive democracy could significantly heighten divisions between social groups; while the legitimation of particular interests or perspectives could mean that no-one tries to see things from anyone else's point of view. What if more care were devoted to ensuring that the parents standing for election as school governors or acting as class representatives or participating in fund-raising activities were themselves roughly representative of the parent body in terms of gender, ethnicity, religion, and class? Though this might curtail the dominance of sub-groups who falsely represent themselves as the voices of the entire community, it also risks encouraging all groups to engage in a special pleading that looks only to their own group's concerns. Working-class parents might then come to see themselves as charged only with promoting the needs of working class children, parents of daughters as charged only with addressing the needs of girls, or parents of black children as speaking only on issues of race. The participation might be equalised, but at the cost of promoting a narrower politics of self or group interest that fails to engage with wider concerns.

So if the first problem with participation is that those who choose to participate are often an unrepresentative sample, the second is that measures to counteract this could lock people more tightly into an interest group politics where everyone becomes exclusively engaged in battling for their own group's concerns. What then happens to deliberation on matters of shared interest? Despite the reservations I have suggested around impartiality, is there not some sense in which we must be willing to recognise that what helps us is not necessarily the best policy, and focus on what is likely to work better for all?

To be genuinely inclusive, participation has to position itself somewhere between two extremes: between the coercive powers of an impartiality that makes it difficult for people to articulate partial experiences and what they know to be group-specific concerns, and the representation of an exclusively group interest that closes them off from alternative points of view. And at its best, this is precisely what most well-intentioned participants attempt to do. They draw, that is, on their own knowledge and experiences and preoccupations to identify gaps in existing practice, but they recognise that their experiences are not the only ones that matter, and try to extend to others the same kind of attention they are claiming for themselves. This, however, is most likely to happen when participants are already drawn from a representative range of different social groups, for it is in these circumstances that people feel most empowered to articulate their specific experiences and most required to consider the implications of experiences that differ from their own. At this point my optimism falters, for while I have enormous confidence in the capacity to deal with difference when that difference is well represented, I am considerably less confident about the prospects of achieving the appropriate balance.

To return to my opening illustrations, the pattern of parental participation is distinctly skewed both within and between schools; and on current indications, the moves to encourage parental involvement seem more likely to increase than reduce inequality. In other contexts, there have been significant attempts to address imbalances in participation by measures of affirmative action. Political parties around the globe have adopted quota measures to increase the representation of women in local and national assemblies; the UK government has recently introduced legislation that makes the use of such measures compatible with anti-discrimination law; while in the USA, the proportion of black representatives was substantially raised by re-districting arrangements that generated constituencies in which black voters formed a voting majority. But no-one has come up with a convincing mechanism that addresses the skewing of representation by class; and no-one (to my knowledge) has proposed the use of formal quotas to address the skewing of participation in schools. As schools become the increasingly hectic site of parental anxiety about their children's progress, it seems absurdly over-optimistic to envisage parental participation as empowering groups of parents whose concerns and preoccupations were not fully served by previous educational practice. When the stakes are so high – and the public funding of education so low – it still looks more likely that participation will become an avenue for (some people's) personal gain.

Note

1 The Education Act (2002) modifies these guidelines, and by 2006 all schools are expected to have adopted a revised model for their governing body. The LEA presence will be reduced to a maximum of one fifth; parents must now make up at least one-third, staff no more than one-third, and community representation at least one-fifth.

6

Home-School Partnerships in Practice

*Barbara M Walker and
Maggie MacLure*

Background

The importance of communication between schools and parents has been a commonplace of educational thinking at least since the Plowden Report (CACE, 1967). However the issue has taken on new inflections following the 1988 Education Reform Act. The restructuring of education as a quasi-market, subject to the mechanisms of choice and accountability, has given parents a new status as consumers, enshrined in the Parent's Charter (DfE, 1991; updated 1994). Such developments have obliged schools to be at least 'attentive' and, where expedient, responsive to parental opinion (Ball, 1994: 1999; Bridges and McLaughlin, 1994). Gerwirtz *et al* note 'semiotic shifts' in the ways in which schools are now representing themselves to their prospective clientele – through the production of glossy brochures for instance, and elaborate 'stage management' of 'promotional events' such as open evenings (1995: 128-9). New forms of parental involvement are also invoked in the home-school 'contracts of partnership' now enshrined in the Government White Paper 'Excellence in Cities' (DfEE, 1998). These formulate joint responsibilities between schools and parents for supporting children's learning (eg Macbeth, 1989; Atkin *et al*, 1988; Tomlinson, 1991).

As Diane Reay has argued (see chapter 2 in this book), whether such developments have actually redressed the power imbalance between schools and homes in educational decision-making is open to question. The reforms have allowed certain parents to exercise their choice of school (eg Ball, 1994), and thus to exert control at the point of 'entry/exit' (Vincent, 1996). And schools may now be more inclined to respond to parental preference when this expresses itself as 'market signals' (Ball, 1994: 99).

However it is unclear to what extent, if any, these systemic changes have influenced the dynamics of communication between teachers and parents. Hancock argues that the Parents' Charter construes parental involvement primarily as the right to information, and thus amounts to 'a one-way accountability exercise in which parents passively listen to what schools are doing rather than engage with teachers to support and influence the content of education' (1993: 17). Home-school agreements have likewise been criticised as less than equitable in their distribution of power, obligation and participation between schools and families. They have been described as protocols for policing parent and child compliance with professional values (Vincent, 1996: 49); as imposing obligations on parents without offering genuine participation (Sallis, 1991: 7); and as a covert selection mechanism for identifying the 'right sort of parents' (Gewirtz *et al*, 1995: 163). More recently, Ouston and Hood (2000) and Hood (2001) concluded from their national survey of teachers, governors, parents and students that the home school agreements do little to improve partnerships between parents and schools and have little impact on those parents who are disconnected from the school.

A more equitable dialogue between parents and teachers is one of the cornerstones of partnership, as envisaged by Bastiani, who proposes, as one defining characteristic, 'A degree of mutuality which begins with the process of listening to each other and incorporates responsive dialogue and 'give and take' on both sides' (1991: 2). While the creation of an equitable and productive dialogue between schools and parents is asserted as a key aspiration of contemporary policy, it is not clear to what extent this aspiration is being met. Indeed, some analysts suggest the education reforms have fractured the moral vision of schools, and depressed the morale of classroom teachers caught between an increasingly managerialist ethos and a more demanding parent body (eg Ball, 1994). We might accordingly expect parent-teacher dialogue to reflect tensions and contradictions rather than mutuality. Or we might anticipate a 'consumerist' trend, involving a heightened attention to children's examination or test performance, and a tendency for parents to express more directly their expectations of teachers' obligations towards their child. It is possible therefore that the changes to the relationship between schools and parents which have taken place at the 'macro' level of systemic reform will have influenced the management of face-to-face encounters, and the distribution of power and dominance in these interactions.

On the other hand, it may be that parent-teacher discourse is quite resistant to change, and that its contemporary forms are little different from those of previous decades, at least in certain interactional contexts. For instance, while schools may be changing their interactional styles on occasions where the recruitment of pupils is at a premium – for instance during 'promotional events', as noted above – older patterns and rituals of interaction, and the power and status relationships that these enact, may prevail during routinised events such as parents' evenings.

The research

This paper draws on two research projects investigating secondary school parents' evenings[1]. These events were chosen since anecdotal evidence suggested that dialogue between parents and teachers becomes more problematic once children entered secondary schooling, and parents' evenings provide one of the main opportunities for such dialogue to take place. In a policy climate which has promoted parental choice, accountability, and shared responsibility between school and home for children's educational and social development, the annual parents' evening is a key event, symbolically at least. They tend to attract higher parental attendance than events such as special subject evenings, sports days, plays, concerts and parent-teacher association social events. However little is known about the nature of the parent-teacher interviews as interactional events.

Trying to throw light into this information black hole, our pilot study, talking to teachers, parents and students (Walker, 1995, 1998) was followed by a larger one funded by the Economic and Social Research Council (MacLure and Walker, 1999, 2000; Walker and MacLure, 1999). Here we observed parents' evenings at five secondary schools where individual teachers and parents audio-recorded their conversations. Four schools were in East Anglia, and one in London. In this study 184 consultations, involving 34 teachers, 126 parents, or other family members and 99 students were made and analysed using discourse analysis techniques developed during research into other professional-client interactions – notably medicine and nursing (eg Mishler, 1984; Fairclough, 1992; Turner, 1995; Silverman, 1987). We also interviewed selected parents, teachers and students after the events.

For those unfamiliar with the UK secondary scene, we begin with a brief description of parents' evenings, which look much the same up and down the country in terms of their overall organisation, although with local variations and innovative formats. The event is often held in the school hall and adjacent communal spaces. Parents, sometimes accompanied by their daughter or son, queue for a series of face-to-face consultations with individual teachers. Consultations are typically scheduled to last five minutes. Usually, an evening is given over to students in a particular year group. So parents of all Year 7s (11 year olds), for instance, will be invited to attend on the same evening. Appointments to see teachers are made in advance by students, on behalf of their parents. An individual teacher may hold 20 or more consultations in an evening; an individual parent or couple may encounter eight or nine teachers.

Parents evenings are, in short, tightly organised, routinised, and often hectic occasions. Some schools are trying to improve the structure, but in general they have changed little since 1981 when Jenny Nias described them as 'a cross between a social security office, a doctor's surgery and King's Cross station'. Another commentator, capturing the sense of dissatisfaction that these events can engender, ranked them 'close to a visit to the dentist in terms of discomfiture' (Limerick, 1987: 52, quoted in Baker and Keogh, 1995: 264).

While the encounters described in this paper all took place within this parents' evening format, we would anticipate that many of the interactional problems are common to other settings where teachers and parents meet to consider the academic and/or general well-being of a student.

Institutional talk

The general characteristics of dialogue in these parents' evenings followed the pattern of 'institutional talk' found in other settings. The most striking similarity was with medical consultations, and this may be because the settings were contextually similar. Such contextual features are associated with interactional patterns which have been described as 'asymmetrical' (eg Ten Have, 1991; Drew and Heritage, 1992): that is, where one participant exerts a greater degree of control over the direction and content of the talk than the other.

For example, in 126 out of a total of the 184 consultations the teacher began with an extended, largely uninterrupted, 'diagnosis' of the student's progress, thus maintaining their 'expert status' and signalling the educationally relevant topics for the rest of the conversation. The teachers also consulted technical resources, such as coursework folders or marksheets, to which parents did not have direct access. This 'diagnosis' would be followed by a dialogue of alternating turns, but parents only entered this phase on invitation from the teacher. Sometimes this was a short passage of agreement, but it was here that some parents attempted to introduce other topics or points of view. However these were frequently overlooked or given minimal acknowledgement by the teacher, who had responsibility for closing the consultation. At times this dialogue could look like a duel, with the teacher attempting to bring the exchange to a close and the parent trying to keep it open.

So the majority of the exchanges recorded confirmed a view of parent's evenings as events over which, 'like the server in tennis, the teacher still has the advantage' (Macbeth, 1989). However some parents did challenge teachers' practice or judgement, and these challenges tended to lead to extended discussions of educational/professional issues such as teaching methods or curriculum plans where the teacher appeared to be justifying their professionalism.

On the page, the majority of these conversations could be described as 'tadpole shaped' with a large head containing the diagnosis, and a dialogic tail of varying length. Alternatively they could be characterised thus:

1. *Preamble* (greetings, orientations, locating markbooks etc)

2. *Diagnosis* (teacher talking, parent(s) acknowledging)

3. *Dialogue* (alternating turns)

4. *Closings* (thanks, farewells etc)

The rest of the chapter focuses on the third phase of the consultation: exploring how phase 3, the dialogue, was conducted.

Securing 'undertakings'

Frequently one or both participants wished for some action to follow up the parents' evening. For instance, parents might be asked to help with homework, see that it was completed, or take action over certain behavioural problems such as lack of concentration, talkativeness, reticence, over-confidence, reluctance to work hard. In general parents acquiesced to these requests and, in the follow-up interviews, three parents remarked that they were pleased to have 'something to do' as a result of the meeting. Alternatively, this acquiescence could be seen as evidence for Edwards and Warin's assertion that home-school partnership has been superceded by the school's colonisation of the home (1999). Certainly these parents were less successful in securing undertakings from teachers, and in some cases had difficulty persuading the teacher to acknowledge that a problem existed. Requests to move students into a different ability group, or to enter them at a higher level GCSE examination were never successful in these consultations, suggesting that teachers' judgments of students' ability were singularly resistant to influence.

However, productive negotiation was possible. One parent who expressed serious concern about other teachers' attitudes to her son, who had previously been excluded from school, secured an undertaking and a date for the teacher to meet privately with the student, to discuss his perceptions of the problem and ways of handling it. One gained the teacher's agreement to do some specific work on study skills, while another obtained an under-taking to provide special help with spelling. Several parents asked teachers to notify them if a problem recurred.

There was some evidence from the follow-up interviews that teachers viewed parental demands as a source of threat and un-predictability. One surveyed the queuing parents with appre-hension: 'You know they have an axe to grind. You just don't know what it is'. Parents who seemed to have 'an agenda' were viewed with some negativity.

Double binds

Although the focus of the consultations was the well-being of the student, teachers and parents found their own identities to be in jeopardy during the exchanges. Parents' evenings stand at the interface between the school and the outside world – a location where the norms and practices of the school are potentially challengeable. So it is hardly surprising that schools wanted to police that boundary, while still needing to subscribe to the rhetoric of parental involvement. Teachers-as-experts were threatened by encounters with adults who could claim to know the children better than they, and who might hold their teaching to account. Parents likewise had their claims to know their chil-dren contested, with the status of parent being undermined by the client role constructed during the event.

Hence it was not a simple matter for the participants to demon-strate competence, maintain a virtuous identity and avoid blame. Both parents and teachers were subject to a number of inter-actional 'double binds' similar to those noted by Silverman in his study of paediatric consultations involving teenagers. Silverman

(1987: 231-2) identified how, in order to prove their competence, parents were obliged to demonstrate that they were acting 'responsibly', by monitoring their child's behaviour, while at the same time helping their child to take control of their own health. So parents resorted to a variety of 'rebuttal strategies' to try to demonstrate competence on one count, without incurring blame on the other.

Parents courted similar risks in consultations with teachers. Showing an interest in students' schoolwork could be seen as exhibiting responsible concern; but it could also be read as being over-protective, or even interfering. One teacher summed up this no-win dilemma in his half-joking description of such parents as 'over protective, deferential or middle class'. This suggests a general dilemma over the notion of parental support for schools. As Crozier (1998: 129) notes, while parental support is universally desired, it can also be perceived as a threat. Hence parents who take an active interest may also be seen as 'watchful'. Support can come to look like counter-surveillance.

A further dilemma encountered by parents related to the triangular nature of the consultation, which always involved three parties, even when the student was not physically present. Parental support for either student or teacher could tacitly be taken as betrayal[2] of the other. So a parent who defended a student in response to teachers' criticism could easily be seen as biased. Some parents were reluctant to take issue with teachers, fearing that such action might rebound on their child. On the other hand, attempting to support the teacher, by backing his or her criticisms of the student, could also be seen in negative ways by teachers – for example as 'ganging up' on the student; or as recruiting teachers against their will to do parents' disciplinary work. One teacher criticised parents who allegedly came to the consultation 'to tell the child off', and who were 'out to just doubly-prove what's gone on at home'. Another teacher was uncomfortable about supporting parents' criticisms of sixth formers: in his view these were responsible young adults, and his relationship with them might be threatened by aligning himself with their parents. Allegiances across the three parties were neither clear cut nor predictable.

The following transcript exemplifies the working of one such double bind. It shows an excerpt from a consultation, together with the teacher's commentary on the extract, made during the follow-up interview.[3] The teacher 'reads' the mother's admonitions to her son as indications of a possible threat to the boy, and as an over-reaction.[4] But it is possible that the mother was attempting to indicate her support for the teacher.

Excerpt from consultation

T I think one of the things, I mean, Chris can be quite good, but I don't think you always give your full concentration, do you? And I think that's one of the problems, I will say

M Yeah

T He tends to drift out and not always be doing, focusing on what is, needs to be done

M Christopher! [sternly]

T And, one of the problems is is you know, you're a bright enough lad, you can do the work, but because we've got such short lessons, I mean they're only an hour long, an hour ten minutes

M Mm

T If you're not focused in or what's happening there and then, and doing it, he gets left behind and not quite finished and quite often you're trying to catch up on work you haven't finished, haven't you? And I think that's where he's got be very careful, he doesn't sort of, slippery slope...

[section omitted]

M Yeah, and especially English, Chris, come on, that's one of the main subjects isn't it?

T And you're quite good at it!

M Yeah

T You know, you can do it, you've proven that in some of the work you've done. You lack concentration a little bit, and you've got to focus on that, OK?

M Who do you sit with on that one? [to C]

C Er, well, either John or Patrick

M Is that him who was down, yeah? Well don't sit near him [continues]

Teacher's commentary on excerpt

Yeah that's right, it was paragraphing [...] And he hadn't bothered. He hadn't listened to what we were doing I think. And I think that's where the concentration came in [...]

Interviewer: Because you make the point lower down [..] 'You're a bright enough lad, you can do the work' [reading from transcript]...

I think that's because Mum told him off. Which comes to the other point I talked about earlier [ie about 'protecting' students from parents' wrath] [...] I mean he tends to drift [...] And mother says 'Christopher!' [...] (So I said) 'Well, Christopher, you're a bright lad' – so Mother gets positive feedback. He's a good boy. Er, that's one of my, yeah, that was because Mum was getting really...angry.

[...]

Mm, I think in the middle of that I've regretted saying he lacks concentration [long extract deleted] sometimes there's no point in going on about the child's achievements because there's going to be – this threatening behaviour that comes through from parents [...] And I could imagine, me reading that, he's quite likely to get a clip round the ear when he gets home

[...]

I mean, truthfully, if you think of what the comment was on concentration, it was looking at a piece of work, so maybe he wasn't concentrating. Not that he lacked concentration every single lesson [...] And she just goes boom! [...] And suddenly it got- the whole thing got swept away in like an area I hadn't anticipated, a very brief comment on a piece of work. And I would have thought, if I'd looked at my notes I would have doubted I had had 'lacks concentration' on my notes

Other examples of teachers' double binds included falling prey to the double imperative of making their subject enjoyable, and thus motivating the student, yet also being expected to push or challenge students. A teacher who claimed to make maths fun, for instance, might be interpreted as making it too easy. The excerpt below indicates a teacher using the 'pedagogical explanation manoeuvre' in response to such a challenge:

> **F** We find that with his homework is, he's finding it relatively easy on the maths side.
>
> **T** The, with homework sheets that I tend to do that, because what I'm wanting them to do, I want the confidence with a lot of them.
>
> **M** Right yes.
>
> **T** And the worksheets that go home, I want them to succeed at, so rather than give them something which they're going to-
>
> **M** – struggle[5].
>
> **T** – for this first term especially, erm, because a lot of them come up to secondary school not liking maths and failing at maths. It's a big thing with them, they come in 'I hate maths, I've always hated maths'. So they get the homework done, where they get lots of ticks-
>
> **M/F** Yes.
>
> **T** – lots of positives. It's alright, it goes in their folder, and they've got ten, or whatever worksheets, it's all correct. It also means that I don't have to spend a lot of time going through that worksheet with them, which I find it demoralises a little bit if they've got crosses on it. They've done it at home, they've tried, with a load of crosses. I think that's awful, because, you know, if they're giving up, they've stopped watching the television to do their homework, they want a success, they don't want something which is going to make them think 'well I'm not going to bother next time, 'cause I'm just going to get it all wrong'. So that's why the homework work sheets tend to be a lot easier than the work I expect them to do in class while I'm there to sort of go through it with them. Erm and it makes them do the homework, it makes them get used to the fact that they're going to get homework. They hand it in on time, they get it marked very quickly, they get an instant result, and it's a pleasing result, so it's a bit of a psychological thing with them and I find that works. Next term things will be different, right, and it will be different for some of them in the groups and you might find that he'll come and say 'well I've got this worksheet and she's got that one and that one's a lot easier', because that's what is going to start to happen.

M Yes.

T At the moment it's lots of photocopiable worksheets, take them home, get them right, get your result, put it in your file, well done. Next term it's going to be yeah you might get some of it wrong, you might struggle a little bit, we'll see how it goes.

Thus teachers could be held responsible for over-estimating, or underestimating, a student's abilities. This double bind was even more acute for teachers of students with special needs, where they felt a responsibility to demonstrate that they were taking special care of special children while at the same time not treating them differently from other children, by lowering their expectations of them.

A further double bind concerned favourable reports of students. Teachers wishing to convey their genuine appreciation of good work might disappoint by failing to demonstrate sufficient engagement with the student, or by telling parents 'what we already know'. On the other hand, teachers could be unwilling to inform parents that their child was doing badly. Often they sympathised with the parents of a poor student, while at the same time wishing to avoid blame themselves.

These studies showed that questions of competence are not settled in advance of consultations. There are no right answers to such questions as how rigorously a 'good' parent needs to monitor homework; where the correct balance lies between fun and pain in the teaching of maths; how much consideration for children with special educational needs is too much or too little; where lines lie between parental concern, interference and deference; who is at fault when a student does not understand. Although parents and teachers may bring their own apprehensions and expectations of each other to the meeting, praise, blame and esteem are traded in the course of the consultations themselves. It is during the consultation itself that conduct comes to be construed as virtuous or blameworthy.

Conclusion
Parent-teacher consultations could be described, somewhat paradoxically, as offering those involved a mixture of predictability and

high uncertainty. On the one hand, they are routinised and formulaic, with teachers seeming to hold the upper hand. On the other, they are fraught with jeopardy and risk of censure for all concerned. While parents' evenings may indeed operate as a surveillance device for monitoring compliance with school values, the surveillance works, in principle at least, both ways. Teachers also render their practices visible and vulnerable to challenge from parents. The relation between teachers and parents (and students) is aptly summarised in Foucault's description of power as 'a mutual and indefinite 'blackmail', which binds superiors and subordinates in 'a relationship of mutual support and conditioning' (1977: 159).

The results of the research problematise policy buzz-words such as 'partnership' and parental 'support'. They suggest for instance that the relations of power and knowledge in these interactions are both highly complex and largely unrecognisable to the participants themselves while they are speaking. Indeed participants' subjectivities as parent or teacher are, in a sense, established through the consultation process itself, in ways that they are not free to alter at will. This is evident in the experience of parents who are also teachers. When such parents attend parents' evenings they experience them emphatically as parents – ie as the relatively powerless actors in the encounter. The participants in institutional 'partnerships' have institutional identities conferred upon them. The notion of parental 'support' is likewise rendered problematic. The multiple perspectives and shifting allegiances that are possible within the triangular relationship of parent, teacher and student create double binds that can transmute competence into culpability. What counts as 'support' in the eyes of one participant may be seen as sucking up, ganging up or surveillance to another.

The combination of straitjacket and uncertainty that haunts consultations makes it difficult to offer general recommendations for improving what are clearly uncomfortable experiences for many, and unproductive for some. It would be possible to derive a list of do's and don'ts from the research. For instance, for teachers: try not to ignore what parents are telling you about the student's personal circumstances; remember that parents may value straight talking over good news; be specific; do not monopolise the conversation. However, such injunctions would be likely to fail, since people may not be able consciously to bend the rules of consultations; and since there is no guarantee in advance as to whether they will emerge as heroes or villains from any particular conversational skirmish.

Acknowledgement

Some data and aspects of this chapter are also incorporated into MacLure, M. and Walker, B. (2003) 'Interrogating the discourse of home-school relations: the case of 'parents evenings' in M. Maclure *Discourse in Educational and Social Research* Buckingham: Open University Press

Notes

1 The second of these studies was supported by the Economic and Social Research Council, award ref. R000222287. See the End of Award Report (MacLure and Walker, 1999) for an account of the methodology and research design.

2 This could be seen by adults as too strong a word, however a sense of betrayal could be keenly felt by students

3 Unfortunately, it was not possible to interview the mother and son involved, so we do not have direct access to their perceptions of the extract. However, the teacher's comments provide a glimpse into how the participants in these consultations might have different interpretations of one anothers' intentions, with clear implications for judgments of 'competence'.

4 Such fears of possible repercussions, which were expressed by other teachers, were offered as one reason why teachers might prefer to avoid giving 'bad news' stories.

5 There were several occasions where, as here, the mother tries to 'smooth' the dialogue, as if finding the father's challenge to the teacher to be too confrontational.

SECTION 3
Participation in Action

7

Parents as citizens: making the case

Carol Vincent and Jane Martin

Introduction

> Parents enter the contested public sphere of public education typically with neither resources nor power. They are usually not welcomed, by schools, to the critical and serious work of rethinking educational structures and practices, and they typically represent a small percent of taxpayers. (Fine, 1997 p.460)

This somewhat pessimistic view of parental participation in schools was put forward by the American sociologist, Michelle Fine, in response to what she saw as a trend in US state education in the 1990s to rally parents to the cause, to involve communities and families in 'fixing' the ills besetting much public education. Basing her arguments on the histories of three parental involvement projects, involving parents from different social class backgrounds, she concludes that if power asymmetries between parents on the one hand and teachers and administrators on the othe, are not addressed, then what emerges are not democratic partnerships between lay and professional actors, but rather projects which seek to educate parents and change their behaviour or at best 'moments [when parents have] a voice but [are] not getting a hearing' (p.473). Such results 'leave neither a legacy of empowerment nor a hint of systemic change' (p.474).

What then is the role for parents in relation to schools and the education system as a whole? What is desirable? What is feasible? What is appropriate? The answers to these questions are all contested.

First of all therefore we start by looking at some of the current responses to these questions drawing on recent research literature, policy and practice. In the second part of this chapter, we offer our own answers, or at least begin to shape some answers. Unsurprisingly, we will argue that there is a role for parents as citizens in their interactions with the education, although the fragility and partiality which besets the manifestations of such a role loom large.

Parental resources

We start by emphasising that parental engagement with education is 'raced', classed and gendered. One example of this is reflected in the frequent use of the stereotype of white middle class parents, intervening in schools, imposing their agenda, and getting what they want. We would challenge such a blanket conceptualisation of middle class agency by pointing to the ways institutions can block parental assertions. As Hallgarten notes, 'although there are clearly class differentials in the parent-school relationship, the feeling of parental powerlessness may actually be the norm....it is almost a case of 'no assertiveness beyond this line' for most parents' (2000 p.28). However, it is clear that parents differ greatly in resources of material, cultural, and social capital; in the quantity of material resources, but also in the nature of the social and cultural resources available to them.

The possession and activation of these resources are extremely influential in determining parental relationship with the school, and the frequency, quality and nature of their interventions. We offer the following example. As part of a recent research project exploring parental voice in schools, and in collaboration with Stewart Ranson, we gathered data concerning the expression of parental voice in schools from a sample of 76 parents from two case study schools. In an effort to gain some analytical purchase on the data we divided the parents into three groupings or cohorts, based on their levels of intervention with the school: high, intermediate and low. The resulting descriptions of parents operating at one of the three levels of intervention are described more fully elsewhere (Vincent and Martin, 2002, Vincent, 2001), but the influence of social class in shaping the behaviour of these cohorts is clear. The high interveners, (27 out of 76) mostly white, higher educated, overwhelmingly homeowners and with a majority employed as public sector professionals, are heavily engaged with the school. They attend general meetings as well as parent-teacher consultations about their own child, and are anxious to monitor closely and supervise their child's progress. The 'low' cohort on the other hand (also 27 out of 76) contains fewer parents with post-16 qualifications, fewer home owners, and nearly half the group (12 out of 27) worked in manual jobs or were long term unemployed (see appendix for details). One of the schools, Willow, was multi-ethnic, and twelve out of the fifteen 'low cohort' parents interviewed there were from minority ethnic groups. All parents in this cohort displayed a discernible reluctance about participating in school meetings. There was a shared feeling that such events were not for 'people like us'. Despite the fact that some of this cohort articulated to us the disappointment and disillusionment they felt with the schools, as well as instances of satisfaction, their behaviour towards the schools was characterised by a 'thundering silence' (Maguire, 2000, personal communication).

If parental involvement with school is not a class-neutral concept, neither is it a gender neutral one. Research on all aspects of parental involvement with school shows that mothers take the responsibility for liasing with the school and also for their child's achievement and progress (choice of school, Gewirtz et al, 1995; contact and communication with school, Vincent, 1996, Reay, 1998, David et al, 1993, Lareau, 1989, Martin and Vincent, 1999, and involvement in the curriculum Merttens and Vass, 1993, Hughes et al, 1994). Yet much of this work is invisible (as are many other aspects of mothering work: see Smith, 1988, 1991, Ribbens 1994, Reay, 1998). Miriam David argues that changes in the structure of families and the increase in maternal employment have in fact led to greater responsibility falling on the mother (David, 1993, see also Anne Phillip's chapter, this volume). The mother is expected to take the key role in and 'total' responsibility (Manicom, 1984, Wyness, 1997) for the development of the child, particularly in his/her early years. This responsibility appears to hold even in dual earner households where mothers are primarily responsible for finding and choosing care and liasing with carers (Brannen and Moss, 1991; Vincent and Ball, 2001, 2003). Mothers, as Walkerdine *et al* (2001) argued, bear the brunt for the social, emotional, moral, intellectual and physical growth of their children (also Edwards, 2002).[1]

There has been surprisingly little UK research on parent teacher relationships conducted with parents from minority ethnic groups, although parent research has often involved mixed race groups (see Vincent, 1996, 2000; Reay, 1998). Exceptions here include the work of Ghazala Bhatti (2000) and Crozier *et al* (2003 and 2004). Bhatti's study of mainly working class Pakistani, Bangladeshi and Indian families reveals the lack of meaningful communication between parents and schools. Parents generally trusted the school but in some cases ended up feeling betrayed and bemused by the school's actions or their children's levels of achievement. Gill Crozier (1996 and chapter 3 in this volume) has also identified distrust and mistrust in relationships between African Caribbean parents and schools.

Parental possibilities

Potential parental roles in relation to schools have been outlined by numerous contributors (Epstein, 1990, Munn, 1993, Woods, 1993, Hughes *et al*, 1994, Desforges with Abouchaar, 2003) including ourselves (Vincent, 1996, Martin, 2000). The labels may vary but the roles in essence we believe are threefold: the partner, the consumer and the citizen.

Partnership

The essence of being a parent 'partner' is, we suggest, support, and this is manifested in two main ways. The first is working with one's own child to support their education, attending parents' evenings and helping with homework being the most obvious examples, but such an involvement may extend to a variety of home-school curriculum schemes, such as SHARE, (Desforges, 2003; Bastiani, 2001; Hallgarten, 2000; see also Dyson and Robson, 1999; Vincent, 1996; Merttens and Vass, 1993). The other strand is supporting the school – 'active volunteerism' (Martin and Vincent, 1999) which entails being an audience at concerts and assemblies, going to and/or arranging a PTA social, helping in the classroom. Teachers often define and sometimes limit parental involvement in and to these terms.

Recently the emphasis on the parental role in the School Effectiveness, School Improvement literature (SESI) has led to developments in the role of parent as partner. As a result of the current emphasis on measuring performance, target setting, and inter school competition for customers, schools have increasingly seen a need to harness and develop parental capacity to work with their children. If parents are, as Shelia Wolfendale (quoting Bloom) characterises them, a 'powerful 'alterable variable'' then co-opting and directing active parental support may well enhance pupil achievement (Wolfendale and Bastiani, 2000).

It is these types of initiative which are well to the fore in a recent school effectiveness and improvement study: *Success Against the Odds – Five Years On* (Maden, 2001). Commenting on the way in which parents were portrayed in the original 1995 volume, Carol Vincent and Sally Tomlinson (1997) argued that

> There was little deviation from the commonplace model of parent-teacher relationships. Parents are audience, volunteers, supporters-from- a-distance; the roles are passive and narrowly defined...Only one narrative mentions the need for teachers to respect parents if the reverse is to be true (Crowcroft Park). Traces of a deficit view of parents remain throughout these accounts, although parents are explicitly seen as part of, or the cause of the 'problem' in just one.' (1997 p.366-7)

Seven years later it appears little has changed in respect of the schools' positioning of parents. The concluding chapter by Margaret Maden speaks of the 'huge boulder of community and parental scepticism and unfamiliarity about education as a personal good' that is evident in some schools (p.310). (An interesting question here is whether she is confusing parental scepticism about particular educational institutions with scepticism about education in general.) The accounts from particular schools concentrate on converting parents into 'contextual factors which support the forward movement of the school' (*ibid*). The emphasis here is clearly on improving measurable performance indicators, and parents are given considerable responsibility in this task. According to one narrative,

> The message to parents is that they are necessary for ensuring the success of the children. The receipt of this message by parents has led to increased support for the aims and aspirations *of the school* for its pupils... the message... [is] that all children could attain level 4 in the core subjects and that parental support on a nightly basis (preferably before the children go out to play) would realise such a target (Evans, in Maden 2001 p.49/50, our emphasis).

There is no sense of sharing or negotiation around the aims of the school here, rather the goal and the means to this end are seen by the school as self-evident, the only difficulty being in ensuring parental compliance. Only one school featured in the collection (again Crowcroft Park) talks of 'discussion' and 'consultation' with parents (pp.83/4).

We suggest that changes in the scope of the parent-as-partner role have not significantly affected the entrenched professional/lay division, nor in some cases the equally entrenched deficit approach to parents. Dyson and Robson (1999) make a similar point in relation to the parental involvement schemes they reviewed (also Desforges, 2003). These schemes are directed towards

> schools in multiply-disadvantaged areas and are targeted at 'needy parents'... we can find little evidence in the literature that parental support is based on any thorough investigation of the actual circumstances of families, the parenting practices within them (including what may be very positive features of those practices) or on any genuinely collaborative attempt at needs analysis. That some of the needs of some parents are being met by such schemes seems beyond doubt. However, the question remains as to whether the needs of the schools may not sometimes take precedence over the needs of families' (p.18) (see also Vincent and

Warren's 1998 account of a parent education group, and Martin and Vincent's 1999 concept of parent 'tutelage').

Parent as consumer

Much has been written about parental responsibility, inclination and capacity to act as consumers of education, making a wise choice of school on behalf of their children (Gewirtz *et al*, 1995, David, 1995, Woods *et al*, 1998, Ball, 2003). Again, a brief summary is necessary here. Consumer action is an individualistic option, one that rests on the supposed power of exit as a sanction (Hirschman, 1970); an argument that presupposes no difference between schools and any other consumer purchase.

> The availability to consumers of the exit option and their frequent resort to it are characteristics of normal competition...the exit option is widely held to be uniquely powerful by inflicting revenue losses on delinquent management. (Hirschman, 1970 p.21)

However, the difficulties that beset parents trying to operate as consumers and enter and exit schools have been well-documented. The practical difficulties of finding alternative places and the emotional upheaval to the family if a change is deemed necessary increases parental anxiety to get the choice right the first time.

Research analysing the effects of choice possibilities in Britain and other western states suggests that allowing parents to choose a school does not necessarily result in greater parental involvement within that school (Goldring, 1997, Whitty *et al*, 1998, Woods *et al*, 1998, Whitty, 2002). Choice does not automatically lead to voice.

> The 'consumer voice' or voices is – or ought to be – an inherent part of (this) political participation. Seeking a place at a preferred school (that is, making a choice in the 'market') is but one action open to parents. This alone does not ensure that they get what they want for their child.(Woods *et al*, 1998 p.201)

The lack of any clear relationship between choice and involvement is conceptual, as well as practical. The archetypal customer, as Bridges and McLaughlin (1994) point out, does not expect their service providers to try and enlist them in the work.

If parents are 'customers', then this suggests that their respon-sibilities are primarily to exercise informed and sensible choice of the school which will provide the educational service. But what of their own educational responsibilities and roles? As customers we expect to employ someone else to get on and do the job for us; we do not expect the plumber to turn round and remind us of the part we have to play in fixing the pipe. (p.76)

Yet, as shown above, schools are generally keen to enlist some measure of parental support and involvement, at least to ensure parents do not retire from the fray once the child is enrolled at school. A model of contractual relations borrowed from the private sector which locates parents purely as consumers, does not fit when applied to public sector schools which demand a more multi-faceted response from parents.

Parent as citizen

Stewart Ranson has argued that '...participation in education can ... help foster not only effective schooling, but also the conditions for a more vital accountability for citizenship' (p.96). It has been argued elsewhere (Martin *et al*, 1996) that education reforms have, in theory, awarded parents the kind of civil and political rights to participate which Marshall (1964) argues are a pre-requisite for citizenship. It is the collective rights of representation on a school governing body which are potentially distinctive about parent-as-citizen, especially as parent governors, since 2003, constitute a third of the total number of places on each governing body. The Standards and Framework Act of 1998 made it a requirement for elected parent-governors to have a seat on local authority committees dealing with education. Although this initiative has been supported by the DfES with the establishment of a national network, early research indicated that without a good deal of support at the local level, parent representatives on such committees remain 'second class citizens' (Martin, 1999a).

Research on parents' roles in governing bodies points to similar conclusions. Whether they have taken up a role as 'active citizens' remains in doubt, despite generally high level of commitment to governorship from parents (Scanlon *et al*, 1999). Deem *et al* (1995) first theorised school governors as active citizens, or rather posed the question as to whether they were empowered citizens or state volunteers.

> We cannot (even) assume that citizenship as evidenced in school governorship is always concerned with public good in civil society. Indeed, as with a number of forms of contemporary citizenship, such as serving on hospital trusts or other semi-public service quangos, school governance of state-funded schools may not be exercised independently of the financial constraints, dominant discourses and policy texts emanating from national states. This may cause us to question whether school governors are indeed acting as empowered citizens in the community or whether they are merely state volunteers. (p157)

However, it has been argued that such a change in culture requires time (Ranson *et al*, 2003). Ranson and his colleagues conclude from their study of governing bodies[2] that although there have always been difficulties in sustaining the flow of lay governors in some areas, the experiment which started in 1986 to encourage some 400,000 volunteer citizens to take part in school governance has to be judged a considerable, though far from complete, success. Whilst they note that 'the under representation of women, ethnic minorities and disadvantaged classes is of continuing concern' their report concludes that 'the largest democratic volunteer force has survived and is beginning to flourish' (Ranson *et al*, 2003, p.4).

Thus there is, to date, some evidence to suggest that some parents at least (largely white and middle class and mostly mothers) are taking up newly accorded rights to participate in school life in the role of citizen, either as governors or as individuals. However, research evidence also suggests that these parents remain in a minority and many others appear to have little appetite for participating in the decision-making of schools as active citizens in the way in which those keen to invigorate the public sphere would advocate (Fielding *et al*, 1991; Hill, 1994; Wright, 1994). Certainly outbreaks of collective parental action are sporadic in the extreme (eg the parents' and teachers' organisation FACE (Fight Against Cuts in Education) which became a major political campaigning group in the 1990s, mobilising against Government attempts to cut the funding for education (Vincent, 2000). The increasing mobilisation of parental pressure groups for children with special educational needs is a more hopeful note, although here the drive to compete for resources can weaken the element of collective action (Martin, 1999b).

Annual Parents' Meetings, one of the initiatives of the 1986 Education Act, legislated for the governing body of all schools to hold meetings open to all parents at which the Governing Body's Annual Report would be discussed. As Thody (1992) comments: 'It's the first time in our political history that there has been a legal requirement to set up a formal means for parents to put their views' (p128). Whilst such a mechanism might in reality amount to little more than a retrospective information giving exercise, there appeared to be potential for increasing parental influence in future school policies and decisions, as the Annual Meeting has the statutory right to pass resolutions (provided the meeting is quorate) of which governors are subsequently required to take note. This opportunity for parents to act as citizens has failed dismally. A Birmingham study (Hinds *et al*, 1992) of the Annual Parents' Meeting verified the lack of enthusiasm on the part of parents for the meeting, demonstrated by poor turn-out at meetings (seldom are meetings quorate thus negating the posibility of passing any resolutions) and by the passive role of most parents who did attend. The study identified:

> ...in nearly half of the cases the parents did not probe any issues arising from the governors' annual report but suggests that parents do know what is important and are at times willing to raise significant issues for discussion about school policies... school management ... curriculum matters... .(p15)

Obstacles to meaningful participation between parents and governors, it was suggested, were caused by the formality of the 'shareholders' business-like AGM model which most schools tended to adopt. A sense of futility was evidenced by parents who had not attended the annual meeting. In the words of one, 'I do not feel it is worthwhile voicing an opinion on school issues when it won't have any effect whatsoever on the way things are done' (p14). Reflecting upon this study, it has been argued (Martin and Ranson, 1994) that the failure of APMs to give parents a collective voice is as much a result of the dominant tradition of profes-sionalism which 'has emphasised the authoritative knowledge of teachers in their practice and the deference of parents as clients' (p202). This is consistent with a civic life which is individualistic and essentially private rather than public. The apparent futility of these meetings was recognised by the Labour Government and since September 2003, exemptions are available to schools, allow-ing them to forgo arranging an APM.

As Carol Vincent (1996) has acknowledged, there are as many problems about the role of parent-as-citizen as there are with parent-as-consumer, particularly given the collective and more public nature of citizenship participation, as compared with the more individualistic and private nature of the consumer-school relationship. It may, in the end, be a case of how the parent voice is expressed in public or in private which is an important signifier of the parent as citizen. As we have suggested (Martin and Vincent, 1999), this will largely depend upon the opportunities provided by the school for parents to have a say, how those oppor-tunities are taken up and by whom.

Building upon the work of Hirschman (1970) we have raised the importance of parents being allowed some space to express their dissatisfaction on behalf of their children, or simply to contribute to decision-making as recipients of a public service. School governing bodies are often cited as the most important example of this and yet all the evidence suggests that lay governors have the most difficulty in making their voice heard (Whitty *et al*, 1998). However, recent studies have reinforced the significance of governors for establishing a collaborative culture for schools improvement (Scanlon *et al*, 1999, Ranson, 2004). Recent research undertaken at the University of Birmingham and referred to above into the impact of school governing bodies on school im-provement and education policy making, investigated the role of volunteer citizens within the broader context of public participa-tion and democratic engagement in local government. Initial find-ings suggest that school governors are playing a significant role as critical friends, in questioning and holding school managers to account, particularly when a school is under-performing.

Whilst we might conclude that an infrastructure has been put in place for parents' rights, particularly those of parent-governor, which would encourage a role for parent as citizen, we have to ask why such 'empowerment' has not generally been supported at the local level nor asserted more robustly by parents themselves. The answer will almost certainly lie in issues around structural inequalities, but also in wider concerns about the nature of both participation and representation in public service delivery at the local level.

Practising citizenship

It might be argued that this status quo is unproblematic, that the above presentation of parent passivity and professional control is a simple result of parents not wishing to exercise voice within schools, and schools not needing their contributions beyond a basic involvement with their own child. Our arguments for changing this situation are twofold. Firstly, for the school to maintain a legitimate and democratic authority, often in a context of difference with a school population marked by social and cultural pluralism, and thus diverse values, priorities and lifestyles, dialogue and negotiation with families is necessary, if the school's authority is to be enhanced, and some consensus reached about its institutional goals. The work of Giddens is relevant here (Giddens, 1991, 1994; Beck et al, 1994). Giddens argues that in late modernity 'expert systems' cannot expect to sustain relationships with passive, dependent clients. With so many sources of knowledge available to lay individuals, a different, more active relationship, one which allows more scope for agency, needs to be constructed. Thus trust between individuals and institutions has to be won by the latter and actively sustained, a process requiring an institutional reflexivity and 'opening-out' to citizens (Beck et al, 1994).

Secondly, education is a key public service and one with fundamental effects on children's life chances. At a time when the local governance of schools is increasingly fragmented, it can be argued that there is a growing need for active public involvement in schools to replace the passive representation of communities through the activities of local education authorities. Only by the establishment and support of intermediary institutions between the family and the state can an associational democracy of in-clusive networks and partnerships be created in which citizens may voluntarily associate to mediate particular and universal interests for the public good (Mouffe, 1993). Not only does this require the local state to acknowledge and support schools as part of such networks but it also needs to support complementary local democratic spaces where local people can exercise their demo-cratic voice and, literally, practice their citizenship. The modernis-ing agenda for local government is beginning to acknowledge this and local authorities are required to consult more broadly and involve local people in decision-making as part of a community planning process leading to a community strategy for the area.[3]

Dialogue and deliberation

We have been involved in two research projects which have sought to consider how parents can exercise a voice in relation to the education system. The first was a project Carol worked on (with Simon Warren) which investigated the experiences, motivations, priorities and actions of parents involved in a variety of grass roots groups organising around educational issues (Vincent, 2000), hereafter referred to as the parent groups project. The second is a project that Jane and Carol worked on together (with Stewart Ranson) which studied the ways in which parents expressed their voice in their children's school, and how schools responded, here-after referred to as the 'voice' project (see Martin and Vincent, 1999; Vincent and Martin, 2002).

For both projects we turned to the literature on citizenship and deliberative democracy to help us understand the problems thrown up by a situation delineated by entrenched professional/lay roles in education and a wider experience of citizen passivity in the public sphere. In an attempt to work through these issues, theorists (e.g. Cohen, 1997; Yeatman, 1994; Young, 1990a; Fraser, 1997; Benhabib, 1996) have been concerned to problematise traditional conceptions of citizenship based upon notions of a universal citizenry with shared values. Such a position ignores both the fractures and cleavages existing amongst different societal groups and the disparities in power and resources that imbue these stratifications. Radical conceptions of citizenship emphasise a re-working of the concept, starting from the contested nature of public purposes and diverse cultural and political identities and values. Through a process of public dialogue, rival positions reach compromises, if not consensus.

We considered the circumstances in which dialogue around educational issues would flourish. What would such forums for dialogue look like? How would they operate? What problems and successes would they experience? There are a number of related concepts here: Nancy Fraser (1997) talks of 'counterpublics', a space and place, an alternative public arena in which members of a subordinate social group could conduct deliberative conversation away from the gaze of the dominant group. This process acts to strengthen the group's abilities to engage with others in the public sphere. Likewise Jayne Mansbridge (1990) talks of 'protected enclaves', and John Keane (1998) of 'micro-public spheres'. In relation to the parents groups project, Carol argues (Vincent, 2000) that 'counterpublics could assist in formulating what Moss (1999 p.80) refers to as a 'politics of parenthood', agendas and priorities that may ultimately support, engage with or contest professional interpretations of the purposes and organisation of schooling'. They could, in short, offer a way in for lay voices struggling to raise educational issues.

In the voice project we used a related concept of 'little polities'. The same notion of a dialogic, deliberative forum features here, but this is one that does not involve complete separation of parents from professional educators. Yeatman's (1994) 'little polities' are described: 'as a collective space for negotiation between public service deliverers and users, as a mechanism for this process' (p88). In our research we considered whether school based parents' forums can be understood in these terms, and whether they have the potential to introduce a 'politics of voice and representation' (Yeatman, 1994, p.110) into state provided welfare services.

The fieldwork

Below we provide some basic information about the projects and then discuss our general conclusions. In the parents' groups project the four groups researched were quite different, their variety being indicative of the way in which parents become involved in educational issues other than or in addition to their relationship with their own child's school. The four case studies were a local authority advice centre for parents of children with special educational needs, a parent education group where parents undertook an accredited practical skills course focusing on making educational materials for young children, a self-help group of African Caribbean parents, and a local branch of a pressure group campaigning for the enhanced funding of education. The study involved some 79 respondents.

The voice project (referred to above) involved six schools, from which three, one primary and two secondary, were chosen for an in-depth study of the school's parent forum, and more generally, to explore the formation and expression of parental voice. Interviews were carried out with 76 families in the two secondary schools, and this number included regular participants in the forums. In the primary school another 20 parents were interviewed.

Our broad conclusions from both projects bore some similarity. There are two points here. The first is that these forums are fragile and partial in their effects. They did offer parents a voice concerning decision-making processes at school and in some cases at LEA level, but they were beset by difficulties, such as the challenge of building up and retaining a healthy membership. As a result core people operated under considerable pressure of work, and maintaining a healthy independent forum was a fraught process. There were instances of professional co-option, whereby parents were not free to determine their own agenda, where discussion was heavily managed, or consultation processes where parental voices were heard but not listened to. Equally there were instances of parental deferral to professional expertise (Martin and Vincent 1999; Vincent and Martin, 2000; Vincent, 2000).

The second point is that because of their fragility, such forums change individuals but not systems. Several individuals who took core roles in one of the parent groups or were closely involved with their children's school clearly benefited in several ways, talking about their enjoyment of their activity, their increased knowledge and confidence. The schools, however and the LEAs with which the forums interacted, continued much as before.

The parents who were involved with these various groups were by no means all middle class, although most were, and few groups included severely disadvantaged families. As we discussed above, secondary school parent-respondents in the parental voice project could be divided into three cohorts – high, intermediate and low – depending on their level of intervention with the school. The experiences, priorities, values and actions of these cohorts are strongly class related, which is unsurprising and unremarkable. Those who are in the least advantaged circumstances are often too concerned with survival issues to have the energy, activity and confidence for interaction with educational institutions.

It seems to us that only by attempting to understand why citizen forums such as the ones discussed here are fragile and partial but nevertheless mostly survive, in these instances anyway, that we can begin to understand how such forums can be supported and encouraged. Such groups are the exception, not the rule. Most of us are not and do not expect to be involved in any type of collective action around public sector services. The explanation for this orientation, this lack of faith in the possibility or utility of collective action can be simply explained: we live in a passive polity. Excavating the reasons for the predominance of a politics of 'domestication, containment and boundary drawing' (Benhabib, 1996a p.7) would require a book. Other chapters in the present collection take up these issues in some ways but here we highlight three relevant points. These are: the relationship between lay persons and professional expertise; class-related strategies of risk management, and the particular and individual nature of many people's motivations to act.

The first point addresses lay individuals' approach to and relationship with apparent sources of expertise invested in professional educators and associated professionals (psychologists for instance). The decline in deference to traditional sources of authority, the proliferation of forms of expertise and competing interpretations of reality from experts within a particular field has, as we noted above, ushered in a more complex relationship between individual and expert. Giddens (1991 p.7) observes that reactions from lay individuals to expert systems draw on a spectrum of possibilities ranging from trust, through pragmatic acceptance and scepticism, to rejection and withdrawal. Nonetheless the proliferation of forms of expertise is still capable of deskilling lay actors, leaving parents uncertain of their right and ability to question or propose change.

However, Giddens also argues that 'the reflexive encounter with expert systems' (1991 p.143) can empower individuals to develop their sense of agency and 'transform the conditions for their own actions' (p.138). He gives the example of a woman with a back problem who becomes aware of the variety of orthodox and alternative treatments available and seeks to inform herself about her complaint and potential remedies in order to make a 'reasonably informed choice' (p.141) about treatment. The exclusivity of such 'reflexive encounters' is clear. The skills and capabilities of reflexivity are unevenly distributed across the population. They are far easier to adopt and practice if one has a range of resources – the money to pay for alternative treatments, the level of education needed to access even popular medical texts, the time to read and digest them, the confidence to question practitioners and so on. All these factors operate to set boundaries on who challenges professionals, who makes their own choices and judgements, and who defers, whatever their degree of scepticism and mistrust.

The second point also takes up class related issues. Bill Jordan and his colleagues have argued that the strategies of risk management employed by middle class groups privilege the household unit over all other forms of collectivity (eg trade unions, local community, collective political action). This prompts particular forms of activity in search of social reproduction and closure (Jordan *et al*, 1994; Jordan, 1996, Ball, 2003). In consequence, some middle class groups seek to handle risks to their household's position strategically and individually, by for example making use of private welfare systems (Jordan, 1996 p.127, Ball, 2003). Those decisions in aggregate can affect a particular area of provision to the extent that not only are groups with fewer social resources excluded, but also the ambitions of the middle classes are vulnerable to frustration. This is partly due to the effects of congestion in particular markets, and the cycle this perpetuates – the continual raising of the stakes. Nevertheless, Jordan argues that with regard to education, the goal of higher education, in a respected institution, cannot be given up – although its attainment cannot be guaranteed – because higher education is seen as the gateway to social reproduction, offering access to a 'good' job and future security and fulfilment. Similarly, Ball *et al* (2002) comment on their study of choice making in HE that,

> As Bourdieu (1988 p.163) suggests, for the privileged classes the hiatus arising between expectation and opportunity, and the concomitant threat of 'downclassing' is 'particularly intolerable' (2002 p.69)

Thus attaining a place at a 'good' secondary school is of supreme importance to most middle class families, and whilst they are generally advantaged and confident as choosers, in this instance many are also 'beset with doubts and loaded with responsibilities' (Ball, 2003 p.171). A dominant concern is to find a school populated by the offspring of 'people like us' (Ball, 2003). Jordan (1996) argues that as a result of the focus and intensity of this choice process, the decisions of the socially advantaged enable the formation of exclusive 'clubs' and mutualities as individuals try to develop assets and resources to best advantage and to manage risk.

The third point addresses the nature and tone of what is deemed to be legitimate for discussion in the public arena. In both research projects we found that the initial motivations of parents to become involved in local groups or school-based parents' forums were informed by the desire to improve or safeguard the education and welfare of their own children. In some cases this concern became generalised to all other children, or to those of a particular group. In other cases the focus remained on an individual child. Such particularity is often deemed to be inappropriate as a spur for participation in public arenas. Birenbaum-Carmeli (1999) argues that self-interest is inevitably selfish and detrimental to deliberation and debate. Similarly, liberal understandings of citizenship often position individuals as 'naturally' possessing the tendency to pursue their own self interest and having to work to 'develop moral capacities to counter their basic selfish acquisitive inclinations' (Dietz, 1992 p.66). Nagel (1991) writes of the extreme difficulties of reconciling the 'duality of standpoints', the 'standpoint of the collectivity with the standpoint of the individual' (p.3). He argues that finding a settlement between personal aims, interests and desires and the ability to abstract oneself from these and recognise that others have equally valid concerns is an unsolved – and largely insoluble – problem. Yet such a solution is the basis of morally acceptable social and political arrangements.

Nagel was not, however, suggesting a binary divide, rather a complex intertwining of the personal and the impersonal. It is on this terrain that another reading of self-interest is possible: self-interest is incomplete as an explanation for participation or, to be more precise, self-interest which is narrowly conceived. As Jayne Mansbridge argues (1990), duty, love (or empathy), two commonly recognised forms of altruism, and self interest intermingle in our actions in ways that are difficult to sort out; 'when people think about what they want, they think about more than just their narrow self-interest. When they define their own interests and when they act to pursue those interests, they often give great weight both to their moral principles and to the interests of others' (1990 p.ix).

Many writers within the (broadly-conceived) deliberative democracy tradition have been concerned to acknowledge, even centre, the importance of the particular and the private in determining what is regarded as legitimate for discussion within the public domain (Young, 1990a, Mouffe, 1993, Fraser, 1997, Phillips, 1999). Sara Ruddick, writing about maternal politics, political motherhood, accepts that this almost always begins with a commitment to a woman's own child and family, and that the movement from one's own to other's children is 'difficult and fragile' (1997 p.374) but possible (also Nagel, 1991). Indeed, she concludes that such particularity is a strength because it acts as a strong source of motivation, as well as being valuable in itself for encouraging empathy.

This passionate particularity is often seen as a limit of maternal politics. 'Real' politics should organise against all injustices; its causes are meant to be transpersonal and transcendent. I, however, see the partiality of maternal politics as part of its promise. People are passionate and local. What looks like the ability to transcend particular attachment is often defensive, self-deceived or the luxury of the strong and safe. Most political relationships have to be created in the midst of passionate particularity, not outside of it. Maternal politics, because it issues out of particular and familiar allegiances, can inspire a move from one's 'own' to 'other', from local to more general. (Ruddick, 1997:p.375)

Suppressing particularity will, as Mansbridge (1990) argues, detract from people's willingness to participate; Nagel's concept of 'duality' illustrates how intertwined the particular and the impersonal standpoints are.

However, it has been argued that it is those parents *already* in a position of social advantage who are using their particularity to consolidate that advantage, and moreover who may have the resources to mask that particularity with a language of universal concern (Birenbaum-Carmelli, 1999). Another disadvantage is that particularity may be used to argue against specific provision on the grounds that 'my' child will not benefit from it. Therefore when the argument is weighed in relation to social justice concerns, it is clear that particularity can sometimes work against the interests of disadvantaged groups as well as sometimes in their favour (Phillips, 1999 p.109-110; Nagel, 1991). However, it is far from clear that prohibiting the expression of particularity is a preferable strategy, as it is one which will lead to a confining, a narrowing of public participation as people direct their energies inwards towards the private household (Vincent, 1992).

To summarise: three reasons are offered here for the existence of 'domestication, containment and boundary-drawing' (Benhabib, 1996 p.7) which act to limit people's public involvement. First, that some sections of the population have few other realistic options but to defer to expert tutelage and guidance. Second, that many middle class households have a tendency to prioritise the individual family over collective strategies. And, third, that particularity – most people's original source of motivation for participation – is often deemed inappropriate as a reason to enter the apparently objective public sphere. Arguably, therefore, the real restraints on active citizenship in education as elsewhere, are those structural social and economic conditions which result in unequal participation, and it is this point we shall dwell on briefly in conclusion.

Conclusion: Unequal participation

In *Which Equalities Matter?*, Anne Phillips (1999) emphasises the material conditions affecting participation and agency. She argues that the current focus on 'equality in the context of difference' (p.9), on gender, racial and cultural hierarchies has, productive and fundamental to the debate though it has proved, 'crowded out older questions of economic equality' (p.14). She argues that people's sense of political competence, efficacy and even of interest in issues decided outside the home cannot be divorced from the economic conditions governing their own lives. There are two issues here – those of access and those of recognition.

> It is not just that the routinised nature of so many people's working lives deprives them of the opportunity to exercise their decision-making powers or that the daily confrontations with poverty leave them no time for political life [access issues]. The deeper problem is that the disparity between rich and poor blocks the recognition of equal worth... the profound lack of social recognition.(Phillips, 1999 p.80)

The lack of social recognition of all citizens is reflected starkly in how people's basic needs are met, the hegemonic positioning of people 'dependent' on state benefits, for example, as 'deficient', both in capabilities and morality. Phillips also refers to David Miller's (1997) argument that social segregation – the isolation of particular class groups in terms of housing, the services used, the schools attended – discourages the capacity to view others as equal; an argument that Jordan (1996) employs in his analogy of 'club-formation', which was mentioned earlier, and is itself a process constructed around an exclusionary imperative.

Our conclusion therefore is largely pessimistic. Although we have identified some potentially positive trends towards the develop-ment of parent-as-citizen – the work of governors, those involved

in parents' groups, and instances of parental voice and engagement in individual schools – we have also identified deeply entrenched inequalities which are resistant to amelioration through
piecemeal initiatives (the hallmark of so much work in the home-
school area, Hallgarten, 2000). Parents will, we suggest, exercise
their agency as active citizens in education, as in other spheres of
citizenship, only when the conditions are created for greater
political and economic equality: a more deliberative society and a
more active and interactive polity with a wider variety of associational groups at all levels.

Notes

1 We note that Edwards (2002) also recognises the significant role of the child in
mediating home and school but have not expanded on this issue within the context of
this paper.

2 ESRC Research Project L215252043 (2000-2002) 'The Participation of Volunteer
Citizens in the Governance of Education' directed by Professor Stewart Ranson with
Dr Margaret Arnott, Dr Jane Martin and Ms Penny McKeown

3 The Local Government Act 2000

Appendix: High, intermediate and low cohorts – the socio-economic breakdown

(Based on a sample group of 76 families).

Occupation

Cohorts	Class 1	Class 2	Class 3	Class 4	Class 5	Totals
High	16	5	2	2	2	27
Intermediate	11	5	3	0	3	22
Low	4	5	2	4	12	27
Totals	31	15	7	6	17	76

Education

Cohorts	Up to 16	Post-16	Degree	Unknown	Totals
High	7	4	7	9*	27
Intermediate	6	7	9	0	22
Low	17	9	1	0	27
Totals	30	20	17	9	76

* The high number of unknowns here is due to the presence in this group of phase 1 forum parents. We did not collect the detailed socio-economic information in phase 1 that we did in phase 2 (although much of it emerged during interview).

Ethnicity

Cohorts	White	African/ Caribbean	South Asian	White other	Totals
High	24	3	0	0	27
Intermediate	16	4	2	0	22
Low	15	4	5	3	27
Totals	55	11	7	3	76

Housing

Cohorts	Owner occupier	Housing association/ council rent	Private rent	Unknown	Totals
High	24	2	0	1	27
Intermediate	19	3	0	0	22
Low	13	9	4	1	27
Totals	56	14	4	2	76

8

Doing Parental Involvement Differently: black women's participation as educators and mothers in black supplementary schooling

Diane Reay and Heidi Safia Mirza

Introduction

Black supplementary schools are set up by and for the black community, and are for the most part self-funding, organic grassroots organisations. These schools which are mainly run by women have a history that reaches back into the 1950s, ever since the first wave of post-war black migrants arrived and settled in Britain (Reay and Mirza, 1997). Unlike the visible, established, voluntary-aided religious ethnic minority schools of the Jewish, Seventh Day Adventist or Muslim community, the schools are difficult to locate as they exist deep within the black community and are hidden away from the public gaze of funders and local authorities. They quietly go about their business in community centres, church halls, empty classrooms, and even the front rooms of dedicated black people.

The schools are small concerns run after school, on Saturdays or Sundays. They are mainly, though not exclusively, for school aged pupils of 5-16. Though some schools could have as few as five pupils, the average school catered for between 30-40 pupils. However popular schools could have as many as 90. As little or no official information is available on these schools, personal and social networks, word of mouth and tracing ads in the black community press yielded our information. In our research we found 60 black supplementary schools in the Inner London and Greater London area where approx 300,000 African Caribbeans live (58.7% of the population). In Lambeth, one of the London boroughs where black people make up almost 30% of the population, we found twelve such schools.

This small scale study of African-Caribbean supplementary schooling focused on just four of the schools, three in London: Colibri, Community Connections and Ohemaa, and one in a provincial city, Scarlet Ibis. To gather qualitative data we carried out participant observation in two of the schools and conducted in-depth interviews with seven black educators involved in running the schools, six women and one man. A repeat interview was later conducted with one of the female black educators. In addition, eight mothers whose children attended two of the supplementary schools were interviewed.

Although all four schools saw their clientele as primarily African-Caribbean this did not mean that the schools were monocultural in terms of their ethnic composition. As one of the black educators pointed out, the schools were culturally diverse in their intake. Only one school saw including white pupils as an acceptable part of their remit, but all accepted African and mixed race students and one had a small number of Asian pupils attending.

Our findings, arising as they do out of a very small scale investigation based on sixteen qualitative interviews and three days of participant observation, are necessarily exploratory and tentative. However, we hope to indicate through our data that black supplementary schools, despite their quiet conformist exterior, contain elements that are both subversive and affirming, providing spaces of radical blackness.

Activism, social capital and black female versions of community

The seven black educators, six women and one man, had been involved in supplementary schooling for periods ranging from four to sixteen years. They had often started out as a member of a small group of black parents, talking in terms of themselves 'and a few other mothers getting together'. Four of the women attributed their initial involvement to their concerns as Black parents with what they perceived to be an uncaring and racist state educational system:

> I got involved as a black parent because I felt the educational system was not operating to a high enough standard to enable my children to realise their full potential. It became manifest when my son came to choose his options and they said he wasn't good enough to do English O level. So first I decided with another couple of mothers that I would tutor our children at home and enter them externally. They all passed and my son got a B. Then it just grew from there with these few parents and me setting up this school. (Maxine, black supplementary school educator)

Charity highlights the gendered nature of many such initiatives:

> It's mainly women who are the ones who are involved in education in this country. Within the Afro-Caribbean community it tends to be mainly women. In my family that was the case and at Colibri it was mainly women who came and that was fine. Obviously, there were a few fathers who were involved and there were a couple of men on the committee but it was mainly women. (Charity, black supplementary school educator)

Charity and Maxine's narratives not only highlight the key contribution of women, they also present a very different version of urban black community to that endemic in popular media and political discourses:

> There was a group of about six parents who, like myself as a Black teacher, were dissatisfied with what was happening to Black pupils. They felt if they had been in the Caribbean their children would be much further on academically and they decided something had to be done, schools weren't doing anything so it had to be them. I really wish someone had the time to chart the enormous amount of work they put in those first few years. It was

immense. The school started off in someone's front room on Saturday mornings. The parents doing all the teaching themselves to start with and it was very much focused on what was their main concern; their children not being able to read and write properly. Then these parents found the group of children grew from 10 to 15 and soon it was 20 and at this point it was unmanageable running a Saturday school in someone's front room so they petitioned the council for accommodation and finally got one of the council's derelict properties. They spent their spare time shovelling rubbish out of the room – tramps had been living there – doing building, repair work, getting groups of parents together to decorate. They pulled together and did all this work themselves, used the expertise they had to get the school on its feet and it was mainly the women organising things, making sure it got done, although in those early days quite a few men were involved as well.

As Charity's words indicate, these four Black supplementary schools generate rich opportunities for contesting prevalent discourses about both contemporary urban communities and inner city working class parental involvement. There is none of the apathy, recalcitrance, fecklessness and aggression which permeate both popular and political discourses of the inner city. Dominant discourses of the urban working class, both black and white, paint pictures of apathetic masses, the inactive and uninformed. Once named 'the underclass' by the socially and politically privileged, and now renamed the 'socially excluded' by the New Labour elite, these urban communities have been ritually pathologised as disengaged, disadvantaged and inherent underachievers (Social Exclusion Unit, 1998). Within these same discourses working class inner city parents are labelled as passive, disconnected, uninterested in their children's schooling.

However both Charity and Maxine tell a very different story; one of effective agency. The agency they speak of is not the individualised agency of the white middle classes (Jordan et al, 1994; Reay, 2003), but rather a collectivised agency grounded in communal responses to a mainstream educational system, which is perceived to be failing black children. In their narratives, and that of Verna quoted below, we hear commitment, reciprocity and continuity:

> I really wanted to do Saturday school because so much was given to me when I was a child. I had so much positive input I wanted to give some of it back. I also wanted to challenge this Government's views on community – that community isn't important. Not that I'm interested in politics. I keep my head down. My work is on the ground with children, doing my bit here and it has been reward-ing, very rewarding. Children have gone through the school that others have given up on and they are doing very well. Matthew who was so very, very difficult when he came, could not sit down for more than thirty seconds, I see him now on his way to college. Perhaps it is alright, you know, that this is a stage. The school has done a great deal for a number of children. I can see the fruits of my labour. (Verna, black supplementary school educator)

Verna is not 'interested in politics'; rather her focus is intensive work 'on the ground with children'. She is engaged in, dare we say, a variant of motherwork (Hill Collins, 1994), but one which, despite her protestations, ultimately has a political edge. Verna's text also speaks of community; a community grounded in her own labour. Community as a concept may be out of favour within academic circles (Young, 1990b), but all the women used the term extensively in their narratives as something they were not simply a part of but were also actively engaged in constructing through their work as educators and parents. As Rose stated emphatically, 'An important part of Saturday school is about creating com-munity. That's part of what we're here for'. Hall *et al* (2002) found a similar commitment to community in their research into supple-mentary schooling in Leeds and Oslo.

In order to make sense of the enormous chasm between popular and elite prejudices in relation to urban communities and the actual practices going on within them we need to inject a gendered analysis (see also Burlet and Reid, 1998). So many successful communities across all fields of society are founded on women's invisible unpaid labour, despite the high profile of male leaders. In her exemplary work on 'reading the community' Valerie Hey dif-ferentiates between male strategies of commandeering social re-sources and female strategies of constructing social capital in order to develop effective community links (Hey, 1998). The black women educators had minimal possibilities of commandeering social resources. Rather, they all worked extraordinarily hard to generate a sense of community and develop social capital out of friends and neighbour social relationships. As Hey succinctly puts it 'there are at least two versions of community – his and hers' (Hey, 98: 2) and these six Saturday schools were all built on 'her' version.

Similarly Patricia Hill Collins makes a case for appreciating the specific nature of black female 'community connectedness'. She suggests we should rearticulate black women's experiences with Afrocentric feminist thought in order to challenge prevailing definitions of community. She writes:

> The definition of community implicit in the market model sees community as arbitrary and fragile, structured fundamentally by competition and domination. In contrast, Afrocentric models stress connections, caring, and personal accountability...Denied access to the podium, black women have been unable to spend time theorising about alternative conceptualisations of community. Instead through daily actions African American women have created alternative communities that empower. (Hill Collins, 1990:223)

Patricia Hill Collins shows that once we re-conceptualise the work of mothers, women educators, church and union leaders, we see that community power is not about domination as in the Eurocentric perspective, but about energy which is fostered by creative acts of resistance. Bourdieu has developed the concept of social capital, which illuminates this point of gendered community participation. He perceives social capital as contacts and group memberships which, through the accumulation of exchanges, obligations and shared identities, provide actual or potential support and access to valued resources (Bourdieu, 1993). Social capital is underpinned by practices of sociability, which require specific skills and dispositions. However, we suggest that there are gender implications that Bourdieu ignores but which would point to a connection between social capital and Helga Nowotny's concept of emotional capital.

Nowotny develops the concept of emotional capital which she defines as 'knowledge, contacts and relations as well as the emotionally valued skills and assets, which hold within any social network characterised at least partly by affective ties' (Nowotny, 1981: 148). As Virginia Morrow points out 'this concept should alert us to the invisibility of women's work in creating and sustaining social networks and hence social capital' (Morrow, 1998: 10). The black women through their involvement as both educators and parents, in supplementary schooling were producing resources to compensate for perceived deficits in state educational provision and thereby enhancing the black community's stock of both social and cultural capital. In 'The Use of Anger: Women responding to Racism' Audre Lorde (1984) links the conceptual and political work of confronting racism with a sense of righteous indignation about 'the way the world is'. It was the positive efficacy of such righteous indignation that both the Black educators and Black mothers demonstrated in their emotional support of Black pupils. As Maxine asserts:

> One of my main aims is to provide a safe space that is both accepting of the child but also provides a challenging context that allows them to grow and realise their potential. I know from my own experience and that of my own children that Black kids constantly get knocked back in ordinary schools, that their confidence gets eroded. I was determined to make sure that never happened in Saturday school.

The Black women educators and mothers appeared to have learnt an awareness of enhancing ways of providing children with emotional support through their own experience of dealing with racism. This paradoxical emotional capital was linked to the social capital many of these women possessed through their community activism and their experiences of returning to study at FE level and in a few cases at the local university. Both capitals emanated from the Black women's 'race' politics and their awareness and experience of related struggle (see also Crozier in chapter 3 of this book).

All six women educators were extensively involved in the wider black community as well as in the community they saw themselves as actively constructing through black supplementary schooling. They were all facilitating black parents' groups and working with local black arts and business collectives. Two of the women were involved in national black women's networks (Sudbury, 1998). The social capital generated through such contacts was fed back into the schools, benefiting the pupils in a variety of ways; through additional funding, sponsorship and curriculum enhancement. For example in Scarlet Ibis a local black business had paid for computing equipment, while members of the black arts collective had volunteered their services and provided sessions on pottery making, set design and printing.

There are a variety of competing tensions in representing black supplementary schools as forms of private sector schooling and evidence of black enterprise. They can be depicted as autonomous self sufficient organisations; part of a vibrant growing largely un-acknowledged black enterprise culture which spans commerce, the voluntary sector, and arts and education fields. Aligned with such understandings of black supplementary schools are views of them as predominantly community self help projects. Such repre-sentations coalesce around new right, and increasingly, New Labour emphases on enterprise and local initiatives. Yet at the same time, there are other images which cut across and powerfully contradict such representations, in particular, black supple-mentary schooling's association with the political Left's project of antiracism and the rediscovery of the histories of marginalised groups'.

Spaces of radical blackness

> White bias is everywhere in education, everywhere except in Saturday school, that is. (Brenda, black parent)

Nancy Fraser writes about 'hidden' public spheres, which have always existed, including women's voluntary associations and working class organisations. In earlier work (Reay and Mirza, 1997) we have argued that there are commonalities between Black supplementary schools and the socialist Sunday schools at the turn of the century. Both constitute 'counter-publics'. Whereas the socialist Sunday schools struggled to produce working class dis-courses to counter hegemonic middle class views on education, black groups in society have repeatedly found it necessary within a wider social context of white hegemony to form 'subaltern counter-publics' in order to signal that they are parallel discursive arenas where members of subordinated social groups invent and circulate counterdiscourses, which in turn permit them to formulate oppositional interpretations of their identities, interests and needs. (Fraser, 1994: 84)

As Fraser goes on to argue, subaltern counter-publics provide spaces of discursive contestation, generating challenges to the discursive *status quo*. On the surface black supplementary schools appear as sites for conformist reinscriptions of dominant discourses, in particular, those of meritocracy and traditional pedagogy. Yet, there exist parallel spaces of contestation within supplementary schooling. In all four black supplementary schools could be found a reworking of dominant discursive notions of blackness. They demark the limits of white hegemony, offering a disruptive discursive space:

I think one of the things we really succeed in is giving the children a positive sense of self. We help them feel comfortable with their blackness when out there they are bound to come up against situations in which they are made to feel uncomfortable about being black. (Verna, black supplementary school educator)

As Verna's words exemplify, in Black supplementary schools can be found a blackness neither vulnerable nor under threat; rather a blackness comfortable with itself. The sense of community evoked by black supplementary schooling aspires to a positive sense of blackness. Other black women educators also gave a sense of supplementary schools as spaces of blackness that held transformative potential for black children:

Our children have said that there's something special about being in an all black environment. It's difficult to explain – that they have this sense of being able tounwind, to be themselves, relax, so that's part of what we provide – a safe environment. (Charity, black supplementary school educator)

As spaces of blackness these four supplementary schools provided their black pupils with familiarity and a sense of centrality often missing from their experience of mainstream schooling. This feeling of comfortable centrality was one in which materiality (the all black context) and the discursive (the valorisation of blackness) were crucially intertwined. Cassie, one of the mothers, powerfully conveys a sense of black supplementary schooling as home:

> The first time I took him to Saturday school it was amazing. We discussed the Saturday school a lot. I saw Saturday school as at times a black home, you know, feeling oh my god I can't cope with looking at a book, 'Oh Akin just go away and read' and I knew that really was not fair to him, he should be able to be motivated all the time. I feel that if someone else is able to do that with him it would be great and I feel the Saturday school will develop that interest in him – the sort of things I'm not able to do because of the pressure on my time. When I came back with him from Saturday school Akin was jumping all over the place and saying 'Mum why can't I go to this school five days a week?' He loved it; he was really really excited. He said I know all about so and so and about so and so, all these people from Black history. He was fascinated and up to now if he's going to do Black history he's really excited. (Cassie, black parent)

In Cassie's words we find a sense of black supplementary schooling as a space of belonging and collectivity. For Cassie black supplementary school represents another home with all the connotations of familiarity and safety that encapsulates. But at the same time she stresses the educational gains. It is both home and school, a combination black children rarely find in mainstream schooling. Black supplementary schools provide places and spaces where blackness becomes a positive and powerful identification, in contrast to mainstream schooling where, regardless of how many anti racist policies are written, blackness is still constructed at best as marginal, at worst as pathological (Gillborn, 1995).

As Verna's, Cassie's and Charity's remarks above illustrate, black supplementary schools provide alternative, autonomous spaces where teachers and pupils can create oppositional and empowering narratives of blackness. Signithia Fordham (1996) has written about the psychological costs incurred when black pupils attempt to achieve academically in mainstream schooling. Because dominant discursive constructions of intellectual ability conflate blackness with being less intelligent she argues that these pupils are forced into a situation where they must 'act white' if they are to succeed, so as not to run the risk of 'liquidating the self'. In contrast, the black supplementary schools were attempting to provide 'sacred black spaces' where children could achieve educationally and still 'act black'.

In recent work bell hooks expresses regret at the passing of separate black spaces, arguing that it has become fashionable to deny any need for black segregation in a world where black people are surrounded by whiteness:

> In the past separate space meant down time, time for recovery and renewal. It was the time to dream resistance, time to theorise, plan, create strategies and go forward. The time to go forward is still upon us and we have long surrendered segregated spaces of radical opposition. (hooks, 1995: 6)

We argue that in black supplementary schooling lie the genesis of hooks' 'segregated spaces of radical opposition'; not in the sense of confrontational male agitation but in a more reflexive, discursive sense. The black women educators were all engaged in various ways in rewriting blackness as a positive social identity in its own right. Such reconstructions, while not oppositional in any traditional sense, are written against the grain of the dominant discursive constructions of blackness as a negative reflection of whiteness which still prevail across British society.

It could be argued that in a key sense black supplementary schools are a response to black people's continuing exclusion from mainstream public spheres which in turn is primarily a consequence of endemic social and institutional racism (Troyna, 1993). Indeed all the black women educators talked about the racism their pupils and their parents encountered outside of the black communities:

> The kids meet so much racism in their everyday lives racism is definitely on the agenda here. We wouldn't be doing our duty by the kids if it wasn't. (Natasha, black supplementary school educator)

Black supplementary schools as 'counter institutional buffers' (Hill Collins, 1990) are not simply defensive institutions – the product of racial oppression which fosters historically concrete communities among black people and other racial and ethnic groups. The black supplementary school is much more than simply a reaction to racism. Like other black community spaces they do not just provide a respite from oppressive situations or retreat from their effects. Rather, as Patricia Hill Collins suggests, 'black female spheres of influence constitute potential sanctuaries where individual black women are nurtured in order to confront oppressive social institutions' (Hill Collins, 1990:223).

In creating a sanctuary in which the black child is recentred, black women decentre the popular pervasive public myth of black underachievement and educational alienation. As radical educators, black women challenge the knowledge claims, pedagogy, and praxis of the mainstream schooling, and harness their own radical version of education as a means of transforming their lives.

However the very thing – spaces of blackness – which make black supplementary schools so inviting for black pupils and the women who create and nurture them constitutes its threat for the white majority. Unlike 'separatist' private independent white schools which are welcomed as standard bearers and examples of good educational practice, black supplementary schools as sites of black solidarity are openly perceived by the white majority as threatening (Tomlinson, 1985).

This threat is conceived on a number of different levels, from crude fears of the 'rising up of the oppressed', to slightly more sophisticated critiques which accept the validity of black supplementary schooling yet criticise them as segregationalist and isolationist. At the heart of this white fear is the simple fact that within black supplementary schools lie powerful evocations of difference and 'otherness' that challenge white dominant hegemonic values. The variety of ways in which black supplementary schools are seen by both the educational establishment and the broader British public raises questions around power, normativity and the endemic terror and fear of blackness that lurks deep within the white psyche (Mirza, 1999).

Doing home-school relations differently?

Supplementary schools operate with a very different home-school interface to mainstream schooling; one in which the parent appeared to remain predominantly the expert on her child, despite the schooling context. However, as is evident in the quote below, sometimes this was at the cost of compromising over what the women educators saw as good educational practice:

> We have spent a lot of time persuading parents how important and educative learning through dance and drama is. However, at the end of the day we have to go with what the parent wants. There is one little boy whose mother insists that he only do Maths and English. I always feel sorry for him when the others go off to do some creative work. But his mother insists so that is that. (Beverley, black supplementary school educator)

Although there is clearly a cost, particularly for this little boy, to giving parents' power, Beverley paints a very different picture of parental involvement to that existing in mainstream schooling where Black and white working-class, and even some middle-class parents, lose their expert status in relation to their child once they enter the school gate. Black educators articulated a keen awareness of the problematic relationship Black parents had with their children's mainstream schools:

> Our parents feel very strongly they are not listened to. The education system has a very long history of keeping parents out. In the 50s and 60s parents had virtually nothing to do with schools. We have come a long way down the road. I think it's part of that history, you know, 'We're the teachers, we know best'. It's partly to do with class but it is also because whenever they see Black parents opening their mouths they see them as creating discord or problems or I can understand the feelings of being fobbed off or not listened to. I think schools need to give more space to parents, to listen to their views. I think there needs to be more links between the home and school. Teachers do not know enough about the context of children's lives and about parents' lives. They need to know and then be able to use that. So I think the relationship between parents and teachers isn't a happy one and it hasn't been for years. It needs developing, it needs encouragement, there needs to be the space for it. (Verna, black supplementary school educator)

This awareness informed their own interaction with parents. Conflicts and tensions, where they did exist, seem to be played out through dialogue rather than the feelings of being 'fobbed off' and not being heard that Black and white working-class mothers re-counted in their tales of mainstream involvement (Reay, 1998; Standing, 1995). However, this is not to deny shades of some of the recurrent tensions between parents and mainstream teachers; namely the construction of parents as a conservative bulwark against innovative practices of educators. Such a perspective is evident in what Beverley, Verna and Natasha say:

> We don't want the situation our parents find in school where they keep on being fobbed off. Here we are very much governed by the parents and what they want. You know they are telling us they don't get listened to in ordinary schools so it is really important that we are seen to listen. But that does cause problems with what we can offer in terms of curriculum because while the staff here would like to give more time to Black studies, parents are telling us to concentrate on the basics, 'to make that your first priority', so in a way there is a conflict, but not really because we have to go with what the parents want. We don't want to make the mistakes of children's ordinary schools so we really prioritise listening to parents. (Natasha, black supplementary school educator)

and:

> Although I have spent a lot of time explaining why we work in the way we do, I suppose the parents could disapprove – in some ways Saturday school is not what they expect. I have a very strong philosophy of child centredness. I have always been very com-mitted to supporting the child. In our society children often don't have a voice. I suppose parents might have expected Saturday school to be more formal, I mean we work in groups, there is no sitting in rows but I believe in working in ways which are best for the child so there is a strong focus on three Rs but also on making the work really interesting for the child, starting from where the child is and integrating things around culture and history. (Verna, black supplementary school educator)

However, there was no uniform parental view among the Black mothers interviewed as to what supplementary schools should teach. Carol, Margaret and Denise see the focus on basics as the main reason for their child's attendance, Anita, Jalil and Elaine see Black history and cultural studies as an equally important an aspect of such schooling while for Cassie it is the most important thing supplementary schools can offer:

Those very things that tackle the identity of children and address their vulnerability as Black people, I think there's going to be less and less of that as the National Curriculum develops because the Government see it as a threat and see it as politics so those teachers who go on doing it are seen as subversive. I think that's the reason they have put this emphasis on parents because they see parents as coming in and taking over from those sort of teachers, teachers who are political. It's an appeal to white parents. That's why I've sent Akin to Saturday school. (Cassie, black parent)

Pedagogic approaches in black supplementary schools

We have examined Black supplementary schools as places for the inscription of positive black identities. We have also seen that in all four schools there were evident tensions in relation to the schools' pedagogic approaches. The four schools all emphasised Black history and Black studies as part of their curriculum offer:

We focus on English and Maths but integrate Black studies into our curriculum offer. For example we'll do a project on black women writers and that will be part of our English curriculum. (Maxine, black supplementary school educator)

But more than that, they offered a space for what Rose called 'thinking black':

You know you've got a maths problem about money and you don't even think about it – it's how much do three yams cost not three pounds of carrots. It's as natural as that just thinking black. (Rose, black supplementary school educator)

While we expected black supplementary schools to generate oppositional discourses on blackness to those prevalent in wider white society, we did not expect our black women educators to espouse child centred philosophies which ran counter to dominant views on pedagogy within the educational field (Reay, 1998b). But they did:

Well we have to be versatile. For example with Shona who teaches here she uses different types of groupwork. She has this group who are very bright and sometimes they'll work together then sometimes she'll put them with the slower children so they can learn from them. We try different ways. And really it is about help-ing these children realise their learning potential because no matter what the experts say, different children have different learning styles, so you can't just use one. You have to keep trying until you find one to suit the child. We are very conscious of that here. We think it's very important to match teaching styles to the child's learning needs. (Maxine, black supplementary school educator)

and:

I have a very strong philosophy of child centredness. I have always been very committed to supporting the child. In our society children often don't have a voice. I suppose parents might have expected Saturday school to be more formal, I mean we work in groups, there is no sitting in rows but I believe in working in ways that are best for the child so there is a strong focus on three Rs but also on making the work really interesting for the child, starting from where the child is and integrating things around culture and history. (Verna, black supplementary school educator)

We are not simply arguing that black supplementary schools are havens of progressive educational practice. However, we suggest that they draw on complex, contradictory pedagogical strands within which childcentredness remains an important component. This is particularly surprising during an historical period in which progressivism has been discredited and superseded within mainstream schooling by more teacher directed approaches which are increasingly reliant on textbooks and whole class teaching. However, as we have already highlighted, this did generate tensions between the desires of some parents and the educational convictions of the women educators. While all seven black teachers, and most of the mothers we interviewed, talked about a productive dialogue between home and school, there still remained strains.

So the women educators' words need to be contextualised within the real tension between the reinscription of traditional curricula through the strong focus on basic skills and the 3 Rs in all four schools, and competing progressive tendencies which prioritised children's initiative and creativity, and their autonomy as learners. All seven black educators were juggling difficult tensions between fitting in with mainstream and their conviction that they could meet the children's needs more effectively. For the black women educators there were additional conflicts both between parental demands and their own educational philosophies, and between their often explicit focus on empowerment and the need to raise educational standards. In all four schools there existed tensions between what the women educators saw as best educational practice and the educational urgency all the black mothers we interviewed felt. This sense of educational urgency, which frequently manifested itself in a demand for the basics, stood in sharp relief to the black women educators' advocacy of a much broader based curriculum.

Our focus is on four schools and we cannot argue that they are typical of black supplementary schooling as a whole. As Sewell's research would seem to indicate, the field of supplementary schooling is characterised by heterogeneity and difference (Sewell, 1996). However, we do argue that our data reveals strands of progressivism and child centredness in all four schools. For example all the schools had a regular circle time and a focus on black studies, while two of the schools had a strong commitment to child centredness that infused all of the curriculum offer. Thus we can say that in marked contrast to mainstream schooling, these black supplementary schools demonstrate in their praxis that high standards, a childcentred approach and a relevant curriculum for black as well as white children are all possible to achieve. They also have a commitment to 'doing parental involvement' very differently to mainstream schooling, despite the tensions sometimes created by listening and responding to what parents felt was best for their children.

Conclusion

In their implicit critique of pervasive unspoken whiteness of mainstream schooling, black supplementary schools put on the historical agenda new problems for society to solve. Black supplementary schools provide a 'sacred space of blackness' (Foley, 1998) that enables the affirming of selfhood that the white majority take for granted in their privileged spaces of whiteness in mainstream schools. The black women educators were all engaged in various ways in rewriting blackness as a positive 'normative' social identity in its own right (see also Mirza, 1997a; 1997b).

Such reconstructions, while not oppositional in any traditional confrontational (masculine) sense, are written in opposition to the dominant discursive constructions of blackness as a negative reflection of whiteness which still prevail across British society.

The women were also reworking notions of community. The sense of community engendered through these black women's activities, embracing as it does an interdependency of the individual and the necessity of the communal, is very different from the traditional notion of community as defined through market forces. The mission of the four supplementary schools in our study is to integrate educational success with a commitment to remaining true to one's origins. On the surface Black supplementary schools appear as sites for conformist reinscriptions of dominant discourses, in particular those of meritocracy and traditional pedagogy. Yet, there exist parallel spaces of contestation within supplementary schooling in which goals of enabling young Black people to achieve academically are combined with a simultaneous opposition to the system, an opposition which is encoded discursively rather than enacted antagonistically, and underpinned by the Black women educators' ceaseless efforts to create oppositional meaning and facilitate social transformation.

9

Conclusion

Gill Crozier and Diane Reay

As many of the chapters in this book demonstrate, parental involvement in its current form is not the uniformly positive good that it is often presented as. Anne Phillips wryly concludes in her chapter in this volume, 'it seems absurdly over-optimistic to envisage parental involvement as empowering those groups of parents whose concerns and preoccupations were not fully served by previous educational practice, especially in a context in which schools have become an increasingly hectic site of parental anxiety about their children's progress' (p96). Bourdieu and Passeron (1979) argue in relation to education that schools recognise and reward the attitudes and practices of the privileged and it is primarily the types of parental participation practised by the white middle classes that are valorised and represented as normative.

In the twenty-first century parental involvement has become the centrepiece in Government policy in education. Myriad government initiatives from school choice to home-school contracts are targeted at parents rather than the pupils. However, far too often parents are perceived either as a homogeneous mass or reduced to a simplistic binary between 'the good' and 'the bad'. As we have said, both approaches neglect complex differentiations of class, ethnicity and gender; in addition the still powerful impact of the economic is ignored, and cultural influences are often reduced to deficit models of working class and minority ethnic parents.

Perhaps one way of avoiding the trap of white middle class norma-tivity, and the judgmental attitudes to anyone positioned as 'other' to that norm which inevitably arise in its wake, is to focus as much on context and family assets as on particular practices. As many of the authors have tried to indicate throughout this book, not just economic, but also levels of cultural and social assets, have power-ful enabling and constraining influences on what parents can do in terms of participating in their children's education. This reality, so often ignored in current Government dictates, makes parental involvement the minefield that many of the chapters in this book expose.

The main themes that emerge out of the book raise key issues in relation to social justice, equality and diversity. Miscommunica-tion between parents and teachers threads its way through most of the chapters. The logocentricity of teachers and schools in terms of their value positions and set agendas is seen to contribute to this. One problem is that schools' agendas are frequently driven by Government policy and in particular the league tables of exam successes and other forms of target setting. Getting parents to comply to support their achievement in these terms is part of this scenario, which leaves little room for addressing the dissonance experienced by many working class and minority ethnic group parents. Many studies have now highlighted this as a key feature of home-school relations but little has yet been done to address it.

Arguably such dissonance is also a consequence of the growing diversity of mass schooling in a hybridised and constantly chang-ing society. It is therefore not an issue that is going to go away. As we noted in our introductory chapter and as indicated throughout this volume, each school will have a different set of circumstances and issues to deal with; therefore addressing the home-school links will be influenced by these conditions. However, common to all must surely be the need to recognise differences in values, attitudes and behaviours amongst their school community and the importance to develop a dialogue on the basis of difference.

A second inter-related theme is differentiation among parents. Not only do the chapters vividly describe inequalities of gender, there are also powerful processes of class and race inequality which can either compound or alleviate those arising from gender. In chapters 1, 2, 5 and 7 in particular, we see how these dimensions constrain parental participation in their children's schools. But we also see that schools are not adept at recognising the barriers to involving parents equitably.

There are issues around how much parental involvement schools want but similarly, according to Jane Ribbens McCarthy (chapter 6), this is also a question concerning parents. She shows how the boundary between the public and the private is one where mothers in particular employ extensive energy to mediate and control. The tension around this boundary is never seemingly resolved but Ribbens McCarthy suggests that perhaps this is one of the key questions which schools and parents ought to negotiate more seriously: that is, where to draw the boundary line.

The investment of emotional work made by parents in their children's education is another recurring theme. Moreover, it is work that goes largely unacknowledged. It is here especially that gender becomes salient. Most of the chapters in this book describe parental participation as a strongly gendered process in which mothers play the central role in supporting their children's education in a variety of ways. That is not to say fathers are disinterested but they tend to be less visible in this respect. Also there is a hidden and at times not so hidden expectation that it is the mother who *should* be the involved parent. Surprising as it may be in the 21st century, there is a residing notion that mothers are always available for child-related duties.

However, inequalities do not arise only from differences between parents. All too often relationships between parents and teachers are defined by their inequitable nature. The power of the professional is clearly depicted in Barbara Walker's and Maggie Maclure's chapter and their analysis of parent-teacher discourse in the parents' evening context. However, Walker and Maclure discuss aspects of the relationship in terms of 'double binds'. As they say, 'Although the focus of the consultations was the well-being of the student, teachers and parents found their own identities to be in jeopardy during the exchanges'(p103). Whilst teachers are under threat of having their expertise challenged, parents, they argue, have their knowledge of their children and thus their role as parent contested. One of the problems in the parent-teacher relationship therefore it would seem, is that the key protagonists do not trust each other.

What we have depicted amounts to a context of high parental anxiety in which Government and many schools operate with a model of parental involvement based on white middle class practice. Within this there is miscommunication, parents who do not fit the norm and parents who have neither the confidence, educational knowledge nor time to participate more fully in their children's school or education generally.

What then can teachers do to improve relationships between home and school? Easy to state but much harder to implement is the importance of recognising the diversity among parents and, in particular, trying to see the world through the eyes of parents who do not fit the norm. This is a wholly different perspective to take from those who patronise parents or see them as inferior. The first hurdle must be to address the diversity of needs represented in the school and deal with the potential conflict of interests this generates. Recent research indicates that white middle class parents are adept at developing strategies that ensure their own children's educational success often at the cost of other, less advantaged children (Ball, 2003; Butler, 2003). So schools need to do all they can 'to level the playing field' by developing forums in which less privileged parents have a voice and can develop some sense of ownership in relation to their children's schooling. In particular, schools could work more closely with community groups and other services now involved in strategies to develop lifelong learning in order to provide help for parents who wish to give their children more support with schoolwork but who find it beyond their own capabilities or knowledge.

Clearly, parent-school relationships are complex and require sensitivity. They do not lend themselves to a wish list of quick fixes; there are no easy answers. And as Basil Bernstein (1970) cautioned over thirty years ago 'school cannot compensate for society'. However, there are still things schools can do to lessen inequalities. Allocating a regular time every week when not only the headteacher but also form and class teachers are available to speak to parents; frequently reminding parents through the newsletter that this is a time when they are welcome to raise concerns; improving signage; ensuring that bilingual assistants are available to welcome minority ethnic group parents; ensuring that the school receptionist has been fully briefed and trained in the parent-school policy requirements – these are just some small but significant considerations that, if not already in place, ought to be adopted. This will not result in a flood of parents who have a history of never coming into school. However, it may convince a few that they are entitled to discuss issues that are worrying them with school staff and it will give the school a more inviting, friendly feel.

We have seen, particularly from the chapters on black parents (Chapters 3 and 8) how important it is to establish an equitable dialogue between parents and teachers. This is particularly crucial in relation to parents with children at risk of being excluded from school. As Gill Crozier's chapter shows, all too often parents are called in too late or when the child has already been excluded. Making early contact with parents of 'at risk' children enables parents to work alongside teachers on developing preventative strategies.

Similarly, encouraging working class and minority ethnic parents to network and develop their own resources of social capital is important. Predominantly middle class schools invariably have their own informal class telephone lists so that parents can regularly contact each other about both social and educational issues. Schools with largely working class intakes could take the initiative in encouraging their parents to network in similar ways. Alistair Macbeth (1995) suggests that setting up such networks which function at the level of the class or year group are less intimidating for white and minority ethnic working-class parents than whole-school parent teacher organisations.

In addition teachers get little or no training in developing home-school links or communicating with parents. Pre and inservice training is therefore urgently needed to address this.

In some respects the overall message regarding democratic parent participation that emerges from these chapters is not optimistic. However, there are some positive examples which provide an indication of what may be possible. Although somewhat cautiously, Carol Vincent and Jane Martin do identify instances of parental voice and engagement, and through the role of the school governors, 'parent as citizen'. And in their chapter on Black Supplementary Schools, Diane Reay and Heidi Safia Mirza show parents and professionals working together in a trusting and equitable way. Thus we have drawn on a range of perspectives and sources of evidence, in an attempt to identify some of the key issues and debates around parental participation in schools. We hope they will shed further light on how to move forward to challenge the inequalities identified and contribute towards a more democratic and inclusive relationship between schools and parents.

References

Ahmad, K. and Bright, M. (2002) Yob Parents Blamed for Child Crime. *The Observer.* 24 March

Apthekar, Bettina (1989) *Tapestries of Life: Women's Work, Women's Consciousness and the Meaning of Daily Experience.* Amherst Massachusetts: University of Massachusetts Press

Arnot, M. David, M.E. and Weiner, G. (1996) Educational Reforms and Gender Equality in Schools. *Research Discussion Series* no 17, Manchester, Equal Opportunities Commission

Arnot, M. David, M.E. and Weiner, G. (1999) *Closing the Gender Gap: Post-war Education and Social Change.* Cambridge: Polity Press

Atkin, J. Bastiani, J. and Goode, J. (1988) *Listening to Parents: an approach to the improvement of home-school relations.* London: Croom Helm

Bagley, C. (1996) Black and white unite or fight? the racialised dimension of schooling and parental choice. *British Educational Research Journal,* 22: 4, 569–580

Baker, C. and Keogh, J. (1995) Accounting for achievement in parent-teacher interviews, *Human Studies,* 18 (2/3) 263-300

Ball, S. (1994) *Education Reform.* Buckingham: Open University

Ball, S. J. (2003) *Class strategies and the Education Market: the middle classes and social advantage.* London: RoutledgeFalmer

Ball, S.J., Davies, J., David, M. and Reay, D. (2002) 'Classification' and 'judgement': social class and the 'cognitive structures' of choice of higher education. *British Journal of Sociology of Education,* 23 (1) pp.51-72.

Ball, S. and Vincent, C. (1998) Grapevine Knowledge. *British Journal of Sociology of Education.* 19 (3): 377-400

Balloch, S. and Taylor, M. (2001) 'Introduction', in Susan Balloch and Marilyn Taylor (eds) *Partnership Working: Policy and Practice.* Bristol: Policy Press

Barnard, N. (1999) The challenge of confrontational parents. *Times Educational Supplement.* 23 April. p 19

Bastiani, J. (1997) *Home School Work in Multi-Cultural Settings.* London: David Fulton

Bastiani, J. (1991) Home-School Contract of Partnership, Home-School Contract of Partnership, *Newsletter* 3, Summer 1991. London: RSA

Bastiani, J. (2001) *Involving Parents in Their Children's Learning: a Framework for Review and Development.* London, London Borough of Tower Hamlets.

Beck, U (1992) *The Risk Society.* London: Sage

Beck, U. Giddens, A., and Lash. S. (eds) (1994) *Reflexive Modernisation: politics, tradition and aesthetics in the modern social order.* Oxford: Polity

Beetham, D., Byrne, I., Ngan, P. and Weir, S. (2002) *Democracy Under Blair: A Democratic Audit of the United Kingdom.* London: Politicos.

Benhabib, S. (ed.) (1996) *Democracy and Difference.* Princeton, NJ: Princeton University Press.

Belenky, M.F., Clinchy, B.M., Goldberger, N.R. and Tarule, J.M. (1986) *Women's Ways of Knowing: The Development of Self, Voice and Mind.* New York: Basic Books

Bell, L. and Ribbens, J. (1994) 'Isolated housewives and complex maternal worlds: The significance of social contacts between women with young children in industrial societies', *Sociological Review,* 42(2): 227-62

Bell, D. (2003) Inequality and Education: Must Urban Schools Fail? Speech given by the Chief Inspector of Schools. Ofsted to the Fabian Society 20th November 2003, London

Bernstein, B. (1970) Education cannot compensate for society. *New Society,* 26 February 1970

Bernstein, B. (1973) *Class, Codes and Control.* London: Paladin Press

Bhatti, G. (2000) *Asian Children at Home and at School.* London: Routledge.

Birenbaum-Carmeli, D. (1999) Parents who get what they want: on the empowerment of the powerful, *Sociological Review,* 47(1): 62-90.

Blackledge, A. (1995) Minority Parents as School Governors in Chicago and Britain: Empowerment or Not? *Educational Review* 47:3: 309-318

Blair, M. and Bourne, J. (2000) *Making the Difference: teaching and learning strategies in successful multi-ethnic schools.* London: DfES, Research Report 59

Bloom, A. (2002) Get Involved, head tells black parents. *Times Educational Supplement* 15 March

Blunden, G. (1983) Typing in the Tec in Gleeson D and Mardle, G (eds) *Further Education* London: Routledge and Kegan Paul

Bourdieu, P (1993) *Sociology in Question.* London: Sage

Bourdieu, P. (1993) *Reflexive Sociology.* Cambridge: Polity Press

Bourdieu, P. (2001) *Masculine Domination.* Cambridge: Polity Press

Bourdieu, P. and Passeron, J. C. (1977) *Reproduction in Education, Society and Culture.* London: Sage

Brain, K and Reid, I (2003) Constructing Parental Involvement in an Education Action Zone: whose need is it meeting? *Educational Studies* 29: 2/3, 291-305

Brannen, J. and Moss, P. (1991) *Managing Mothers: Dual Earner Households After Maternity Leave.* London: Unwin Hyman.

Bridges, D and McLaughlin, R. (eds) (1994) *Education and the Market Place.* London: Falmer

Bristol Women's Studies Group (1979; 1984) *Half the Sky: an introduction to women's studies.* London Virago

Brown, A. (1993) Participation, Dialogue and the Reproduction of Social Inequalities in R. Merrtens and J. Vass (ed.) *Partnerships in Maths: Parents and Schools.* London: Falmer

Brown, P. (1990) The 'third wave': education and the ideology of parentocracy. *British Journal of Sociology of Education,* 11: 1, 65-85.

Burlet, Stacey and Reid, Helen (1998) 'A gendered uprising: political representation and minority ethnic communities'. *Ethnic and Racial Studies* 21:2, 270-287

Burman, E. (1994) *Deconstructing Developmental Psychology.* London: Routledge

Butler, T. with Robson, G. (2003) *London Calling: The Middle Classes and the Re-Making of Inner*. London Oxford: Berg

Central Advisory Council for Education (CACE) (1967) *Children and their Primary Schools (The Plowden Report)*. London: HMSO

Clarke, J. and Glendinning, C. (2002) 'Partnership and the remaking of welfare governance', in Glendinning, C., Powell, M. and Rummery, K. (eds) *Partnerships, New Labour and the Governance of Welfare*, Bristol: Policy Press

Cohen, J. (1997) Deliberation and deliberative democracy, in Bohman, J. and Rehg, W. (eds.) *Deliberative Democracy*. Cambridge, Mass: MIT.

Coleman, J.S. (1997) *Social Capital*. New York Basic Books

Crozier, G. (1998) Parents and schools: partnership or surveillance? *Journal of Education Policy*, 13 (1), pp. 125-136

Crozier, G. (1996) Black Parents and School relationships: a case study. *Educational Review*, 48:3, 253-266

Crozier, Gill (1997) 'Empowering the powerful: a discussion of the interrelation of government policies and consumerism with social class factors and the impact of this upon parental interventions in their children's schooling', *British Journal of Sociology of Education*, 18 (2): 187-200

Crozier, G. (2000) *Parents and Schools: Partners or Protagonists?* Stoke on Trent: Trentham Books

Crozier, G. (2003) Researching Black Parents: making sense of the role of research and the researcher. *Qualitative Research*, 3:1, 79-94

Crozier, G., Davies, J., Khatun, S. and Booth, D. (2003) School, Family and Community Relationships: the impact of tradition, culture and values on home-school relationships, with reference to families of Bangladeshi origin in the North East of England. British Educational Research Association Annual Conference. Herriot Watt University September 2003 and www.edu-online@leeds.ac.uk

Crozier, G. and Davies, J. (2004) School Relationships with Pakistani and Bangladeshi Parents: what can be done to maximise involvement? American Educational Research Association Annual Meeting. San Diego, April 12

Curthoys, A. (2000) Adventures of Feminism: Simone de Beauvoir's Autobiographies, Women's Liberation and Self-Fashioning. *Feminist Review* 64, Spring pp 3-18

David, M.E. (1980) *The State, the Family and Education*. London: Routledge

David, M.E. (1993) *Parents, Gender and Education Reform*. Cambridge Polity Press

David, M.E. (1995) 'Parental wishes versus parental choice' *History of Education* 24 (3): 267-276

David, M.E. (1999) Home, Work, Families and Children: New Labour, New Directions and New Dilemmas in *International Studies in the Sociology of Education*. 9 (3): 209-229

David, M.E. (2002) From Keighley to Keele: personal reflections on a circuitous journey through education, family, feminism and policy sociology. *British Journal of Sociology of Education*. 23 (2): 249-269

David, M.E. (2003) *Personal and Political: Feminisms, Sociology and Family Life*. Stoke on Trent: Trentham Books

David, M.E., Alldred, P. and Edwards, R. (2001) Children and School-based Research: 'Informed Consent' or 'Educated Consent'? *British Educational Research Journal*. 27 (3): 347-365

David, M.E. and Woodward, D. (1998) (eds) *Negotiating the Glass Ceiling: Senior Women in the Academic World*. London: Falmer Press

David M.E., Ball S.J., Davies, J. and D. Reay (2003) Gender Issues in Parental Involvement in Student Choices of Higher Education. *Gender and Education.* 15 (1): 21–37

David, M.E., Davies, J., Edwards, R., Reay, D. and Standing, K. (1996) Mothering, Reflexivity and Feminist Methodology in Morley L and Walsh V (eds) *Breaking Boundaries:Women in Higher Education.* London: Taylor and Francis

David, M.E., Davies, J., Edwards, R., Reay, D. and Standing, K. (1997) 'Choice within Constraints: Mothers and Schooling' in *Gender and Education.* 9 (4): 397-410

David, M.E., Edwards, R. Hughes, M. and Ribbens, J. (1993) *Mothers and Education: Inside Out? Exploring Family Education Policy and Experience.* London: Macmillan

David, M.E., West, A. and Ribbens, J. (1994) *Mother's Intuition? Choosing Secondary Schools.* London: Falmer Press

David, M. E., West, A., Noden, P., Edge, A. and Davies, J. (1997) Parental Choice, Involvement and Expectations of Achievement in Education. London School of Economics, Centre for Educational Research *Clare Market paper* 13 p16

Davidoff, L. (1990) 'Adam spoke first and named the orders of the World': masculine and feminine domains in history and sociology', in Helen Corr and Lynn Jamieson (eds) *The Politics of Everyday Life: Continuity and Change in Work and the Family.* London: Macmillan.

Davidoff, L., L'Esperance, J. and Newby, H. (1976) 'Landscape with figures: home and community in English society'. In Mitchell, J. and Oakley, A. (eds) *The Rights and Wrongs of Women.* Harmondsworth: Penguin.

Deem, R. Brehony, K. and Heath, S. (1995) *Active Citizenship and the Governing of Schools.* Buckingham: Open University Press

Department of Education and Science (DES) (1985) *Better Schools: A White Paper.* London: HMSO

Department of Education and Science (DES) (1986) *Education Act.* London: HMSO

Department of Education and Science (DES) (1988) *Education Reform Act.* London: HMSO

Department for Education (DfE) (1992) *Choice and Diversity.* London: HMSO

Department for Education (1994) *Our Children's Education: the updated parents' charter.* London: HMSO

Department for Education and Employment (DfEE) (1997) *Excellence in Schools.* London: HMSO

Department for Education and Employment (DfEE) (1998a) *Excellence in Cities.* London: HMSO

Department for Education and Employment (1998b) *Draft Guidance on Home-School Agreements.* London: Department for Education and Employment

Department for Education and Employment (1998c) *Homework Guidelines for Primary/ Secondary Schools.* London: Department for Education and Employment

Department for Education and Employment ((1998) *Excellence in Cities.* London: HMSO

Department for Education and Skills (2003) *Aiming High: Raising the Achievement of Minority Ethnic Pupils.* London: Department for Education and Skills

Desforges, C. with Albouchaar, A. (2003) The Impact of Parental Involvement, Parental Support and Family Education on Pupil Achievement and Adjustment: A Review of the Literature. *Research report* No. 433. London: DfES.

Dietz, M. (1992) Context is all: feminism and theories of citizenship. In C. Mouffe (ed.) *Dimensions of Radical Democracy.* London: Verso.

Drew, P. and Heritage, J. (Eds) (1992) *Talk at Work: interaction in institutional settings.* Cambridge: Cambridge University Press

Duncan, S. and Edwards, R. (eds) (1997) *Single Mothers in an International Context: Mothers or Workers?* London: UCL Press

Duncan, S, and Edwards, R. (1999) *Lone Mothers: Paid Work and Gendered Moral Rationalities.* London: Macmillan

Dyer, C. (2003) Mother Loses Truancy Challenge. *The Guardian.* 8 March

Dyson, A. and Robson, E. (1999) *School, Family and Community.* York: Joseph Rowntree Foundation.

Edwards, A. and Warin, J. (1999) Parental involvement in raising the achievement of primary school pupils: Why bother? *Oxford Review of Education*, 25(3): 325-341

Edwards, R. (1993a) *Mature Women Students: Separating or Connecting Family and Education.* London: Taylor and Francis

Edwards, R. (1993b) 'The university' and 'the university of life': boundaries between ways of knowing', in David, M., Hughes, M., Edwards, R. and Ribbens, J. *Mothers and Education: Inside Out? Exploring Family-Education Policy and Experience.* Basingstoke: Macmillan

Edwards, R. (ed.) (2002) *Children, Home and School: Regulation, Autonomy or Connection?* London: RoutledgeFalmer

Edwards, R. and Alldred, P. (2000) 'A typology of parental involvement in education centring on children and young people: negotiating familialisation, institutionalisation and individualism.' *British Journal of Sociology of Education*, 21(3) 435-455

Edwards, R. and Ribbens, J. (1998) 'Living on the edges: public knowledge, private lives and personal experience', in Ribbens, J. and Edwards, R. (eds) *Feminist Dilemmas in Qualitative Research: Public Knowledge and Private Lives.* London: Sage

Ehrenreich, B (1990) *Fear of falling: the inner life of the middle classes.* New York: Harper Perennial

Epstein, J. L. (1990) 'School and family connections: theory, research and implications for integrating sociologies of education and family' in D. G. Unger and M. B. Sussman, *Families in Community Settings: Interdisciplinary Perspectives.* New York: Haworth Press

Fairclough, R. (1992) *Discourse and Social Change.* Cambridge: Polity Press

Fairclough, N. (2000) *New Labour, New Language?* Harlow: Longman

Fielding, N., Reeve, G. and Simey, M. (1991) *Active Citizens: New Voices and Values.* London: Bedford Square Press

Fine, M. (1997) [Ap]parent involvement: reflections on parents, power, and urban public schools. In A. Halsey, H. Lauder, P. Brown and A. Stuart-Wells (eds.) *Education, Culture, Economy and Society.* Oxford: Oxford University Press.

Freeman, J. (1985) *The Tyranny of Structurelessness.* London: DarkStar/Rebel Press (first published 1970)

Foley, Douglas, (1998) 'Review Symposium; Blacked Out: Dilemmas of Race, Identity and Success at Capital High'. *'Race' Ethnicity and Education* 1 (1):131-135

Fordham, Signithia (1996) *Blacked-Out: Dilemmas of Race, Identity and Success at Capital High.* Chicago: University of Chicago Press

Foucault, M. (1977) *Discipline and Punish.* London: Penguin

Fraser, N. (1994) Rethinking the public sphere: a contribution to the critique of actually existing democracy. In H. A. Giroux and P. McLaren (eds) *Between Borders: Pedagogy and the Politics of Cultural Studies.* New York: Routledge. pp 74- 98

Fraser, N. (1997) *Justice Interruptus: critical reflections on the post-socialist condition.* New York and London Rutledge

Galton, M., Simon, B. and Croll, P. (1980) *Inside the Primary Classroom.* London: Routledge and Kegan Paul

Galton, M. (1989) *Teaching in the Primary School.* London: David Fulton

Gaskin, K. and Davis Smith, J. (1997) *A New Civic Europe? A Study of the Extent and Role of Volunteering.* London: The National Centre for Volunteering

Gewirtz, S., Ball, S.J., Bowe, R.(1995) *Markets, Choice and Equity.* Buckingham: Open University Press

Giddens, A. (1991) *Modernity and Self-Identity: Self and Society in the Late Modern Age.* Oxford: Polity

Giddens, A. (1992) *The Transformation of Intimacy: Sexuality, Love and Eroticism in Modern Societies.* Cambridge: Polity Press

Giddens, A. (1994) 'Living in a post-traditional society' in U. Beck, A. Giddens, and S. Lash *Reflexive Modernisation: politics, tradition and aesthetics in the modern social order.* Cambridge: Polity Press

Gillan, A. Prison Worked, Says Truants' Mother. *The Guardian.* 27 May

Gillborn, D. (1995) *Racism and Anti-racism in Real Schools.* Buckingham: Open University Press

Gillborn, D. and Youdell, D. (2000) *Rationing Education: Policy, Practice, Reform and Equity.* Buckingham: Open University Press

Gilkes, Cheryl Townsend (1983) 'From Slavery to Social Welfare: Racism and the Control of Black Women'. In Amy Swerdlow and Hanna Lessinger (editors) *Class, Race and Sex: The Dynamics of Control.*Boston: Hall. pp 288-300

Gillies, V., Ribbens McCarthy, J. and Holland, J. (2001) *Pulling Together, Pulling Apart: The Family Lives of Young People,* London: Joseph Rowntree Foundation/Family Policy Studies Centre

Glatter, R., Woods, P., and Bagley, C. (1997) *Choice and Diversity in Schooling.* London: Routledge.

Goldring, E. (1997) Parental involvement and school choice: Israel and the United States, in R.Glatter, P. Woods, and C. Bagley (1997) *Choice and Diversity in Schooling.* London: Routledge.

Gordon, L. (1980) *Family Planning in the USA.* Harmondsworth: Penguin

Habermas, J. (1996) *Between Facts and Norms.* Cambridge: Polity Press

Hall, K., Ozerk, K., Zulliqar, M. and Tan, J. (2002) 'This is our school': provision, purpose and pedagogy of supplementary schooling in Leeds and Oslo. *British Educational Research Journal.*28 (3): 399-418

Hallam, S. and Cowan, R. (2000) Is Homework Important for Increasing Educational Attainment? http://www.ioe.ac.uk/teepwdj/lde_online.htm

Hallam, S. (2004) *Homework: The Evidence.* London: Institute of Education

Hallgarten, J. (2000) *Parents Exist, OK?* London: IPPR.

Halsey, A. H. (1972) (ed) *Educational Priority, vol 1: EPA Problems and Policies.* London: HMSO

Hancock, R. (1993) Professional language, literature and parents. *Language Matters.* 3: 16-19

Hartsock, N. (1998) *The Feminist Standpoint Revisited and other essays.* Boulder Colorado and Oxford: Westview Press

Hey, V. (1998) Reading the Community: A critique of some post/modern narratives about citizenship and civil society. In P. Bagguley and G. Hearn (eds) *Transforming the Political.* London: Macmillan

Hill, D.M. (1994) *Citizens and Cities – Urban Policy in the 1990s.* Hertfordshire: Harvester Wheatsheaf

Hill Collins, P. (1990) *Black Feminist Thought: Knowledge, Consciousness and the Politics of Empowerment.* London: Routledge.

Hill Collins, P. (1994) 'Shifting the Center: Race, class and feminist theorising about motherhood. In D. Bassin, M.Honey and M.M.Kaplan (eds) *Representations of Motherhood.* New Haven: Yale University Press

Hill Collins, P. (1998) *Fighting Words. Black Women and the Search for Justice.* Minneapolis and London: University of Minnesota

Hill Collins, P. (2000) *Black Feminist Thought.* London: Routledge

Hinds, T., Martin, J., Ranson, S. and Rutherford, D. (1992) The Annual Parents Meeting: Towards a Shared Understanding, a Project Report to the Department for Education

Hirschman A. (1970) *Exit, Voice and Loyalty.* Cambridge: Harvard University Press

Hochschild, A. (1983) *The Managed Heart.* Berkeley and LA: University of California Press

Hood, S. (2001) Home-School Agreements: a true partnership? *School Leadership Management.* 21:1 pp7-17

hooks, bell (1995) *Killing Rage: Ending Racism.* London: Penguin Books

Hughes, M. and Kennedy, M. (1985) *New Futures: Changing Women's Education.* London: Routledge

Hughes, M., Wikely, F. and Nash, T. (1994) *Parents and their Children's Schools.* Oxford: Blackwell

Irvine, J. (1990) 'Black Parents' Perceptions of their Children's Desegregated School Experiences.' Paper presented at the annual meeting of the American Educational Research Association, Boston, Massachucetts, April. Cited in G. Ladson-Billings (1994) *The Dream Keepers.* San Fransisco: Jossey-Bass Publishers

James, N. (1989) Emotional Labour. *Sociological Review.* 37 (1): 15-42

Jellison Holme, J. (2002) Buying Homes, Buying Schools: School Choice and Social Construction of School Quality. *Harvard Educational Review* 72 (2): 177-205

Jordan, B., Redley, M. and James, S. (1994) *Putting the Family First: Identities, Decisions, Citizenship.* London: UCL Press

Jordan, B. (1996) *A Theory of Poverty and Social Exclusion.* Cambridge: Polity Press.

Keane, J. (1998) *Civil Society: Old Images, New Visions.* Cambridge: Polity Press.

Kenway J, S., Willis, S., Blackmore, J. and Rennie, L. (1998) *Answering Back: Girls, Boys and Feminism in Schools.* London: Allen and Unwin

Kirkpatrick, S. (2000) Mothers' Relationship with their Children's Primary Schools – A Limited Partnership? Dissertation presented for the MA in Family Research, Oxford Brookes University

Kralovec, E. and Buell, J. (2000) *The End of Homework: How Homework Disrupts Families, Overburdens Children, and Limits Learning.* Boston: Beacon Press

Kralovec, E. and Buell, J. (2001) 'End homework now', *Educational Leadership,* 58 (7): 39-42

Ladson-Billings, G. (1994) *The Dream Keepers.* San Fransisco: Jossey-Bass Publishers

Lareau, A. (1989) *Home Advantage.* London: Falmer Press

Levin, I., Levy-Shiff, R., Appelbaum-Peled, T., Katz, I. and KomarNachshon Meiran, M. (1997) 'Antecedents and consequences of maternal involvement in children's homework: a longitudinal analysis', *Journal of Applied Developmental Psychology,* 18(2): 207-227

Lorde, A (1984) *Sister/Outsider: Essays and Speeches.* NY: The Crossing Press Inc

Lucey, H. and Reay, D. (2000) Social Class and the Psyche. *Soundings* issue 15: 139-154

Lucey, H. and Reay, D. (2002) 'Carrying the beacon of excellence: pupil performance, gender and social class. *Journal of Education Policy* 17 (3): 321-336

Luttrell, W. (1997) *Schoolsmart and Motherwise.* London and New York: Routledge

Luttrell, W. (2003) *Pregnant Bodies: Fertile Minds.* New York and London: Routledge

Mac an Ghaill, M. (1988) *Young, Gifted and Black.* Buckingham and Philadelphia: Open University Press

Macbeth, A. (1989) *Involving Parents: Effective Parent-Teacher Relations.* Oxford: Heinemann Educational

Macbeth, A. (1995) Partnership between parents and teachers in education in Macbeth, A., McCreath, D. and J. Aitchison (eds) *Collaborate or Compete? Educational Partnerships in a Market Economy.* London: Falmer Press

MacLure, M. and Walker, B. (1999) Brief Encounters of a Predictable Kind. *Managing Schools Today.* 8 (9): 52-54

MacLure, M. and Walker, B. (2000) Disenchanted Evenings: The Social Organisation of Talk in Parent-Teacher Consultations in UK Secondary Schools. *British Journal of Sociology of Education.* 21 (1): 5-25

Maden, J. (ed.) (2001) *Success Against the Odds – Five Years On.* London: Routledge

Manicom, A. (1984) Feminist frameworks and teacher education. *Journal of Education,* 166: 77-102.

Mansbridge, J. (1980) *Beyond Adversary Democracy.* New York: Basic Books

Mansbridge, J. (1990) *Beyond Self Interest.* Chicago: University of Chicago Press.

Marquand, D. (1997) *The New Reckoning: Capitalism, States and Citizens.* Cambridge: Polity Press

Marshall, G. Swift, A. and Roberts, S. (1997) *Against the Odds? Social Class and Social Justice in Industrial Societies.* Oxford: Clarendon Press

Martin, J. (2000) The changing practice of parent-school relations: a tradition contested Unpublished PhD thesis: The University of Birmingham

Martin, J. (1999a) 'Social justice, education policy and the role of parents: a question of choice or voice? *Education and Social Justice* 1(2): 48-61

Martin, J. (1999b) 'Parents' organisations: single interest or common good?' in H. Daniels (ed) *Special Education Reformed: Shaping the Future.* London:Falmer .

Martin, J. and Ranson, S. (1994) 'An opportunity for partnership: Annual Parents' Meetings' in A. Thody *Moving to Management: School Governors in the 1990s.* London: David Fulton

Martin, J., Ranson, S., Nixon, J. and McKeown, P. (1996) School governance for the civil society; redefining the boundary between school and parents'. *Local Government Studies* 22(4): 210-228

Martin, J. and Vincent, C. (1999) Parental voice: an exploration International Studies in *Sociology of Education,* 9 (3): 231-252

Massey, R. (1993) *Parent Power: Securing the Best Schooling for Your Child.* Cambridge Press: Harmsworth

Mayall, B. (1994) 'Children in action at home and school'. In Berry Mayall (ed) *Children's Childhoods Observed and Experienced.* London: Falmer Press

Mayall, B. and Foster, M-C. (1989) *Child Health Care: Living with Children, Working with Children.* Oxford: Heinemann

McGrath, D.J. and Kuriloff, P.J. (1999) 'They're going to tear the doors off this place': upper-middle class parent school involvement and the educational opportunities of other people's children. *Educational Policy.* 13 (5): 603-629

McKie, Linda, Gregory, Susan, and Bowlby, Sophia (2002) 'Shadow times: the temporal and spatial frameworks and experiences of caring and working'. *Sociology,* 36(4): 897-924

McNamara, O., Hustler, D., Stronach, I., Rodrigo, M., Beresford, E. and Botcherby, S. (2000) Room to manoeuvre: mobilising the 'active partner' in home-school relations. *British Educational Research Journal* 26 (4): 473-490

Merttens, R. and Vass, J. (eds) (1993) *Partnership in Maths: Parents and Schools.* London: Falmer Press

Miller, D. (1997) 'What kind of equality should the left pursue?' In J. Frankin (ed.) *Equality.* London: IPPR

Mirza, H.S. (1997a) 'Black Women in Education; a collective movement for social change'. In H.S Mirza (ed) *Black British Feminism.* London: Routledge

Mirza, H.S. (1997b) 'Mapping a Genealogy of Black British Feminism' in H.S Mirza (ed) *Black British Feminism.* London: Routledge

Mirza, H.S. (1999) 'Black Masculinity and Schooling: a Black feminist response'. *British Journal of Sociology of Education* 20(1): 137-147

Mishler, E. (1984) *The Discourse of Medicine: Dialectics of Medical Interviews.* New Jersey: Ablex

Morrow, V. (1999) Conceptualising Social Capital in relation to Health and Well-being for Children and Young People: a critical review. *Sociological Review.* 47 (4): 744-765

Moss, P. (1999) Going critical. In S. Wolfendale and H. Einzig (eds.) *Parenting Education and Support.* London: David Fulton.

Mouffe, C. (1993) *The Return of the Political.* London: Verso

Munn, P. (1993) *Parents and Schools – Customers, Managers or Partners?* London: Routledge

Nagel, T. (1991) *Equality and Partiality.* Oxford: Oxford University Press.

New, C. and David, M.E. (1985) *For the Children's Sake: Making Child Care More than Women's Business.* London: Penguin

Nias, J. (1981) Highstones: mirror images and reflections'. In J. Nias, *Case Studies in School Accountability. Vol II* (Cambridge Accountability Project)

Nowotny, H. (1981) 'Women in Public Life in Austria'. In Cynthia Fuchs Epstein and Rose Laub Coser (eds) *Access to Power: Cross-National Studies of Women and Elites.* London: George Allen and Unwin

Oakley, A. (1974) *Housewife.* Middlesex: Penguin

Office For Standards In Education (1994) *Reporting Pupils' Achievements.* London: HMSO

Office For Standards In Education (1995) *Guidance on the Inspection of Nursery and Primary Schools.* London: HMSO

Ouston, J. and Hood, S. (2000) *Home-School Agreements: a true partnership? Report of a research project for the Research and Information on State Education Trust.* London: RISE

Parry, G. Moyser, G. and Day, N. (1992) *Political Participation and Democracy in Britain.* Cambridge: Cambridge University Press

Porter, M. and Porter, F. (1999) Making New Feminisms: A conversation between a Feminist Mother and Daughter. *Feminist Voices.* No 6

Phillips, A. (1991) *Engendering Democracy.* Cambridge: Polity Press

Phillips, A. (1995) *The Politics of Presence: Political Representation by Gender, Ethnicity and Race.* Oxford: University Press

Phillips, A. (1999) *Which Equalities Matter?* Cambridge: Polity Press.

Putnam, R. (2000) *Bowling Alone: the Collapse and Revival of American Communites.* New York: Simon and Schuster

Ramirez, A. (2003) Dismay and Disappointment: parental involvement of Latino immigrant parents. *The Urban Review* 35 (2): 93-110

Ranson, S. (2004, forthcoming) Configuring school and community for learning: the role of governance. *The London Review of Education Journal*

Ranson, S., Arnott, A., Martin, J. and McKeown, P. (2003) *The Participation of Volunteer Citizens in the Governance of Education. Final report to the ESRC*

Rawls, J. (1971) *A Theory of Justice.* Oxford: Oxford University Press

Reay, D and S, J Ball (1997) 'Spoilt for choice': The working classes and education markets'. *Oxford Review of Education* 23 (1): 89–101

Reay, D (1998a) *Class Work: Mothers' Involvement in their Children's Primary Schooling.* London: University College Press

Reay, D (1998b) Setting the agenda: the growing impact of market forces on pupil grouping in British secondary schooling. *Journal of Curriculum Studies* 30 (5): 545– 558

Reay, D (2000a) A useful extension of Bourdieu's conceptual framework?: Emotional capital as a way of understanding mothers' involvement in children's schooling. *Sociological Review.* 48 (4): 568-585

Reay, D. (2000b) A Useful Extension of Bourdieu's Conceptual Framework: emotional capital as a way of understanding mothers' involvement in their children's education? *The Sociological Review.* 568-585

Reay, D. (2003) Reproduction, reproduction, reproduction: Troubling dominant discourses on education and social class in the UK. In J. Freeman-Moir and A. Scott (eds) *Yesterday's Dreams: International and Critical Perspectives on Education and Social Class.* New Zealand: University of Canterbury Press

Reay, D. and Lucey, H. (2003) The limits of choice: Children and inner city schooling *Sociology.* 37 (1): 121-142

Reay, D. (forthcoming) Many Roughs and Toughs: Class, Race and Representation in the inner city. *Sociology*

Reay, D. and Mirza, H. (1997) 'Uncovering Genealogies of the margins: Black Supplementary Schooling'. *British Journal of Sociology of Education* 18 (4): 477-499

Reay, D., Ball, S.J. , David, M.E. and Davies, J. (2000) Student Choices of Degree or Degrees of Choice? Race and the Higher Education Choice Process. *Sociology.* 35 (4): 855–874

Reynolds, D. and Cuttance, P. (1992) *School Effectiveness: Research, Policy and Practice.* London: Cassell

Ribbens, J. (1992) Mothers with Young Children: Responsibility with or without Authority? Paper presented to the *British Sociological Association Annual Conference,* April, University of Kent

Ribbens, J. (1993) 'Having a word with the teacher: ongoing negotiations across home-school boundaries'. In David, M.E., Hughes, M., Edwards, R. and Ribbens, J. *Mothers and Education: Inside Out? Exploring Family-Education Policy and Experience.* Basing-stoke, Hants: Macmillan

Ribbens, J. (1994) *Mothers and their Children: A Feminist Sociology of Childrearing.* London: Sage

Ribbens, J. and Edwards, R. (1995) 'Introducing qualitative research on women in families and households'. *Women's Studies International Forum*, 18(3) 247-58

Ribbens McCarthy, J., Chalcraft, D., and Edwards, R. (1999) Gendered Lives, Gendered Concepts? The Significance of Children for Theorising 'Public' and 'Private'. Paper presented to the British Sociological Association Annual Conference, April, University of Glasgow

Ribbens, J. and Edwards, R. (eds) (1998) *Feminist Dilemmas in Qualitative Research: Public Knowledge and Private Lives.* London: Sage

Ribbens McCarthy, J. and Edwards, R. (2000) 'Moral Tales of the Child and the Adult: narratives of contemporary family lives under changing circumstances', *Sociology.* 34(4):785-804.

Ribbens McCarthy, J. and Edwards, R. (2001) 'Illuminating meanings of 'the private' in sociological thought: a response to Joe Bailey'. *Sociology*, 35(3): 765-777

Ribbens McCarthy, J. and Edwards, R. (2002) 'The individual in public and private: the significance of mothers and children'. In Carling, A., Duncan, S. and Edwards, R. (eds) *Analysing Families: Morality and Rationality in Policy and Practice.* London: Routledge

Ribbens McCarthy, J., Edwards, R. and Gillies, V. (2003) *Making Families: Moral Tales of Parenting and Step-Parenting.* Durham: Sociology Press

Rose, N. (1990) *Governing the Soul: The Shaping of the Private Self.* London: Routledge

Ruddick, S. (1997) Rethinking maternal politics. In A. Jetter, A. Orleck, and D. Taylor (eds.) *The Politics of Motherhood.* Hanover. NH: University Press of New England

Sallis, J. (1991) Home/school contracts: a personal view. Parents in a Learning Society. *Royal Society of Arts News.* 4: 7

Sartori, G. (1987) *The Theory of Democracy Revisited: Part One: The Contemporary Debate.* London: Chatham House

Scanlon, M., Earley, P. and Evans, J. (1999) *Improving the Effectiveness of School Governing Bodies, Research Report RR111,* Suffolk: DfEE

Sewell, T. (1996) South London supplementary/heritage schools: shifting out of dominance. Paper presented at *British Educational Research Association Conference.* Lancaster University. September

Sewell, T. (2002) Challenging Cultures – changing schools. Conference presentation. *Whose Schools? Whose Rules?* organised by The 1990 Trust part of the and Runnymede Trust, Derby.

Seyd, P. and Whiteley, P. (1992) *Labour's Grass Roots: the Politics of Party Membership.* Oxford: Clarendon Press

Sharma, U. and Black, P. (2001) Look Good, Feel Better: Beauty Therapy as Emotional Labour. *Sociology.* 35 (4): 913-931

Silverman, D. (1987) *Communication and Medical Practice.* London: Sage

Sieber, T.R. (1982) The politics of middle class success in an inner-city public school. *Boston University Journal of Education,* 164 (1): 30-47

Smith, D.E. (1987) *The Everyday World as Problematic: A Feminist Sociology.* Milton Keynes: Open University Press

Smith, D. (1991) Writing women's experiences into social science. *Feminism and Psychology.* 1 (1): 155-169.

Smith, D. and Griffith, A. (1990) Coordinating the Uncoordinated: Mothering, schooling and the family wage. *Perspectives on Social Problem.* 24 (1): 25-43

Social Exclusion Unit (1998) *Bringing Britian Together: A national strategy for neighbourhood renewal.* Report by the Social Exclusion Unit Cmd 4045 London, HMSO

Solomon, Y., Warin, J. and Lewis, C. (2002) Helping with homework? Homework as a site of tension for parents and teenagers. *British Educational Research Journal*, 28(4): 603-622

Standing, K (1997) Scrimping, Saving and Schooling: lone mothers and 'choice' in education. *Critical Social Policy*. 17(2): 79-99

Standing, K (1999) Lone Mothers and Parental Involvement: A Contradiction in Policy? *Journal of Social Policy* 28 (3): 479-497

Stanley E (1992) *The Auto/Biographical I*. Manchester: Manchester University Press

Strauss, A. and Corbin, J. (1990) *Basics of Qualitative Research: grounded theory procedures and techniques*. London: Sage Publications

Strong, P. (1979) *The Ceremonial Order of the Clinic*. London: Routledge

Sudbury, J. (1998) *'Other Kinds of Dreams': Black women's organisations and the politics of transformation*. London: Routledge

Ten Have, P. (1991) Talk and institution: a reconsideration of the 'asymmetry' of doctor-patient interaction In D. Boden and D.W. Zimmerman (Eds) *Talk and Social Structure: studies in ethnomethodology and conversation analysis*. Cambridge: Polity Press

Thody, A. (1992) *Moving to Management: School Governors in the 1990s*. London: David Fulton

Thrupp, M. (2000) *Schools Making a Difference. Let's Be Realistic*. Buckingham and Philadelphia: Open Univeristy Press

Tomlinson, S. (1985) The 'Black Education' Movement. In M. Arnot (ed) *Race and Gender*. Oxford: Pergamon Press

Tomlinson, S. (1991) Home-school partnerships. In S. Tomlinson and A. Ross (eds) *Teachers and Parents*. London: IPPR.

Topping, K. (1996) The effectiveness of family literacy in S. Wolfendale and K. Topping (eds) *Family Involvement in Literacy*. London: Cassell

Troyna, Barry (1993) *Racism and Education: Research Perspectives*. Buckingham: Open University Press

Trustram, M. (1984) *Women of the Regiment: Marriage and the Victorian Army*. Cambridge: Cambridge University Press

Turner, B.S. (1995) *Medical Power and Social Knowledge*. (2nd ed) London: Sage

Vetta, A. Slow Fuse for Minefield. Opinion, *Times Educational Supplement*, 29/3/02

Vincent, C. (1992) Tolerating intolerance? Parental choice and race relations the Cleveland case, *Journal of Education Policy* 7 (5): 429-443

Vincent, C. (1996) *Parents and Teachers: Power and Participation*. London: Falmer

Vincent, C. (2000) *Including Parents? Education, Citizenship and Parental Agency*. Buckingham: Open University Press

Vincent, C. (2001) Social class and parental agency, *Journal of Education Policy* 16 (4): 347-364

Vincent, C. and Ball, S. (2001) A market in love? Choosing pre-school child care, *British Educational Research Journal*, 27, (5): 633-651.

Vincent, C. and Ball, S.J. (2003) Metropolitan Mothers: Mothers, mothering and paid work, Paper presented at British Educational Research Association conference. Herriott-Watt University, September.

Vincent, C. and Martin, J. (2002) Class, culture and agency: researching parental voice. *Discourse* 23 (1):109-128.

Vincent C. and Tomlinson, S. (1997) Home-school relationships: the swarming of disciplinary mechanisms? *British Educational Research Journal*, 23 (3): 361-377.

Vincent, C. and Warren, S. (1998) Becoming a 'better' parent? Motherhood, education and transition, *British Journal of Sociology of Education*, 19 (2):177-193.

Vincent, C and Warren, S. (2000) Class, race and collective action in J. Salisbury and S. Riddell (eds) *Gender, Policy and Educational Change: Shifting Agendas in the UK and Europe*. London: Routledge

Walker, B. (1995) Evenings of our discontent. *Times Educational Supplement*, 27 October

Walker, B. (1998) Meetings Without Communication. *British Educational Research Journal* 24 (2): 163-178

Walker, B. and MacLure, M. (1999) M. Parents Get Tail End of the Talk. *Times Educational Supplement*, 14 May

Walkerdine, V (1997) *Daddy's Girl: Young Girls and Popular Culture*. London Macmillan

Walkerdine, V., Lucey, H. and Melody, J. (2001) *Growing Up Girl: Psychosocial Explorations*. London: Palgrave Macmillan.

Wallman, Sandra (1978) 'The boundaries of 'race': processes of ethnicity in England'. *Man*. 13(2): 200-217

Ward, L. (2003) Parents of Holiday Truants Face £100 Fine. *The Guardian* 27 December

Weeks, J., Donovan, C. and Heaphy, B. (1999) *Families of Choice*. Harmondsworth, Middlesex: Penguin/Polity

Whitty, G., Power, S. and Halpin, D. (1998) *Devolution and Choice in Education: The School, the State and the Market*. Buckingham: Open University Press

Whitty, G. (2002) *Making Sense of Education Policy*. London: Paul Chapman

Wolfendale, S. and Bastiani, J. (2000) *The Contribution of Parents to School Effectiveness*. London: David Fulton.

Woods, P. (1993) 'Parents as consumer-citizens'. In R. Merttens and J. Vass, (eds) *Partnership in Maths: Parents and Schools*. London: Falmer Press

Woods, P., Bagley, C. and Glatter, R. (1998) *School Choice and Competition*. London: Routledge

Workshop on Partnership with Parents (1997) Primary Headteachers Conference, Leadership and Learning, 6th-7th March, *Essex County Council*

Wright, C. (1992) *Race Relations in the Primary School*. London: David Fulton

Wright, T. (1994) *Citizens and Subjects – An Essay on British Politics*. London: Routledge

Wyness, M. (1997) Parental responsibilities, social policy and the maintenance of boundaries, *The Sociological Review*, 45 (2): 304-324

Yeatman, A. (1994) *Postmodern Revisionings of the Political*. London: Routledge.

Young, I.M. (1990a) *Justice and The Politics of Difference*. Princeton NJ: Princeton University Press

Young, I.M. (1990b) 'The Ideal of Community and the Politics of Difference'. In Linda Nicolson (ed) *Feminism/Postmodernism*. London: Routledge

Index

'race' xi, 6, 15, 24, 26, 35,
37, 40-41, 45-46,
87, 89, 95, 114, 116,
138
– equality 157
– politics 143
racism 43-47, 55, 143
– anti 144
– institutional 147
repair work 32, 140
representation xiii, 83-86,
94-96, 144120-121,
124, 126, 144
rights 4, 12-121,

self-interest 35-36, 93,
130-131
school governors 95, 120-
121, 123
social capital 20, 46, 88,
114, 139, 141, 144,
159
social class ix, xi, 17, 36,
41, 43, 87-88, 115
social reproduction 27,
33-36, 129, 130
social science 5, 14-15,
18
solidarity 148

spaces
– of blackness xiv,
145-148
– of contestation
138, 145, 154
– segregation 35,
147
– of whiteness 153
status 45, 83, 97, 99, 103
status quo 37, 43, 55, 93-
94, 124, 145
Standards Task Force viii
Standards and
Framework Act viii
surveillance 53, 69, 104,
109

Teacher Training Agency
(TTA) 39
trust xi, 51, 118, 124,
129, 158, 160

volunteering 87

whiteness 147, 153-154
– white x, 27, 41-44,
46-48, 54, 61, 89,
114-115, 121, 138,
140, 144, 146, 148,
150-156, 158-159

working class
– the 140
– children 95
– community 13
– mothers 150
– organisations 144
– parents 27, 46, 95,
116, 140, 149, 156,
159
– pupils 85

UNIVERSITY OF PLYMOUTH
LIBRARY SERVICES (EXMOUTH)
DOUGLAS AVENUE
EXMOUTH
DEVON EX8 2AT